W9-ANU-668

PREPARING FOR THE SACRAMENT OF MARRIAGE

PREPARING FOR
THE SACRAMENT OF
MARRIAGE

Dr. Anthony & Mary Del Vecchio

Ave Maria Press ● Notre Dame, Indiana 46556

First printing, July, 1980
Sixth printing, April, 1996
70,000 copies in print

Nihil Obstat:
    Rev. David A. Dillon
    Censor Librorum/Deputatus

Imprimatur:
    †John R. Roach, D.D.
      Archbishop of St. Paul and Minneapolis

© 1980 by Ave Maria Press, Notre Dame, Indiana 46556

All rights reserved. No portion of this book may be reproduced in any form without the written permission of the publisher.

Library of Congress Catalog Card Number: 80-67721
International Standard Book Number: 0-87793-208-5

Art and cover design by Joyce Stanley DePalma
Manufactured in the United States of America.

Contents

Preface

Dr. Anthony and Mrs. Mary Del Vecchio have been coming to the Diocese of Gary for several years to conduct psychological seminars aimed at assisting priests to get to know themselves better in order that they could more efficaciously relate to each other and become more inspirational in their ministering to the people whom they are privileged to serve. In the course of these seminars, the priests noted the definite effectiveness of Dr. Del Vecchio's techniques in the promotion of self-knowledge and the necessity for self-discipline which prompted them to seek his advice on ways and means to apply some of his methods to the solution of some of the personality problems of their parishioners.

Marital difficulties that disturbed families, broke up marriages and shattered tranquility proved to be the most numerous. This caused the priests and Dr. Del Vecchio to focus their attention on the reasons for these marital problems in order to solve them or better yet how to prevent them in the first place.

To this end, from January through August in 1977, a model course of preparation for marriage was inaugurated differing from the usual Pre-Cana Conference.

The reactions of the couples completing the model preparation for marriage course were so positive that in September, 1977, the Pre-Cana was dropped entirely and the Catholic Marriage Preparation Course developed by the Del Vecchios instituted.

Since September, 1977, through April 13, 1980, thirty-seven weekend courses were offered for 1300 couples. Since not all couples can make this course, a comparable course is being offered in the diocese which, since 1978, has been taken by 254 couples.

It is still too early to evaluate the precise and lasting effectiveness of this marriage preparation course now preferentially promoted in the diocese and favorably accepted by the parish priests who regard it as a valuable asset in their pastoral concern for the establishment of happy families.

One indicator of the effectiveness of this course may be the decision of some couples to postpone their wedding date for a while; another, the decision of some couples to simply part company. . . decisions based on what they discovered about themselves through the course.

An institution as essential to a sane, happy and secure way of family life as is the married state needs to have its dignity recognized and highly revered. Unless the married state can maintain an aura of sacredness and stability about itself, it can easily deteriorate into an affair of selfish expedience.

Couples preparing to accept each other as husband and wife need to realize that the distinctive, unifying bond of partnership which the sacrament of matrimony will fashion out of them and which they alone will administer to each other is something holy, something touched with the divine, something indissoluble.

In modern society's prevalent climate of permissiveness in which there is little regard for the sacred, the sacrificial, the permanent, it may not be easy for engaged couples to reveal their true personalities to each other openly, genuinely and without any reservations. This kind of self-revelation is a definite necessity for the sincerely honest acceptance of each other as husband and wife in a spirit of total, unconditional, personal surrender to the ideal of a glorious, glowing union and partnership immune to any challenges to its integrity and beautiful togetherness.

Deeply involved with the Del Vecchios in the premarital instruction program is Father John Siekierski, vicar of the Marriage Tribunal for the Diocese of Gary. They form a strong, committed, confident and able group which, with the aid of several other dedicated persons, is planting the seed for an abundance of positive good in the growth of happy families.

It is our prayerful hope that the utilization of these guidelines and techniques will enable engaged couples to prepare themselves so conscientiously for life together as husband and wife that the result will be the multiplication of loving, prosperous families which will enhance and strengthen the nation, and spread the Good News as they reflect the comforting joy and radiant light of the Lord.

Andrew G. Grutka
Bishop of Gary

Introduction

Congratulations! You have found the person with whom you wish to share your love, your dreams, your hopes, your talents and your desires for the rest of your life.

Better yet, you have courageously promised to be true to each other, to be loving, and to make your union permanent. And you have chosen to celebrate this commitment through the sacrament of matrimony.

You are probably concerned about how you can fulfill this commitment when you are surrounded by glamorized lifestyles detrimental to permanent marriage—lifestyles that advocate living together "with all the advantages of marriage and none of the disadvantages," lifestyles that do not advocate the value of marital fidelity. You must contend with the popular notion that "until death do us part" is old-fashioned, unrealistic and boring.

In addition, significant role changes for adults have added even more pressure to the marriage commitment. Traditionally the husband was seen as the head of the family, the breadwinner, the disciplinarian; the wife was seen as the heart of the family, the child-rearer, the homemaker. These roles no longer prevail, primarily because of a sexual revolution and the two-paycheck family.

Finally, divorce statistics show that within five years one-third of you who are now renting halls and hiring caterers will be facing each other in divorce courts. With such overwhelming statistics, you may be asking, "How can I have a permanent, sacramental marriage that will fit into modern society?" You get the feeling you are out of step simply because you believe marriage is for keeps.

We do not believe that in choosing a sacramental marriage you are bucking a trend that looks upon marriage as an institution on the way out. Our 30 years' experience as marriage counselors, lecturers and seminar leaders tells us a different story. Young couples become engaged and get married because they believe that marriage can be a lifestyle for happiness and self-fulfillment, and be permanent.

This book intends to give you the direction needed to fulfill your wedding-day dreams of a permanent relationship. You will come to understand how your values and your needs give direction to your behavior. You will learn about values that are important to a successful marriage, about needs and how they can help or hinder you. It will also hopefully show you how *being real*, *being understanding* and *being caring* are processes that create the best conditions for a happy marriage.

Using this material we have conducted marriage preparation courses for several thousand couples. The participants tell us that knowing their own values and understanding their partner's values makes being real, understanding and caring much easier. They find there is much less need to be defensive, that they can be more open, more willing to take risks. They experience more closeness, more growth and more self-fulfillment.

From our interaction with the participants in our marriage preparation programs, we have found that the following questions contain key points to help determine whether or not you are prepared to make a permanent commitment:

1) **How well do I really know myself?**

2) **How well do I really know my partner?**

3) **Does my partner see me the way I see myself?**

4) **Am I being real? In other words, is my behavior consistent with what I understand about myself (my self-image)?**

5) **Do I fully realize that mutual understanding is a cornerstone for marriage—an art that I can develop through practice?**

6) **Do I know what it means to be warm and caring toward my partner without the need to dominate?**

7) **Do I understand how the church's teaching on family life can fit into a modern marriage?**

If you feel that these questions are important and you wish to pursue the sacrament of matrimony, we truly believe that this book can be a starting point for a happy married life. It offers guidelines for a permanent, sacramental marriage that will help you cope with contemporary lifestyles. It is directed toward helping you achieve the following goals:

1) **a permanent marriage**

2) **a marriage in which fidelity is a cornerstone,**

3) **a relationship that is a source of mutual love and procreation.**

That's what it's all about—how to live a happy married life by following the teachings of the church in a covenant of matrimony. We hope to help your head take over the tasks that are opened up by your heart. Happy marriage to you! And now let's explore the ways in which you can make marriage the greatest adventure of your lives.

How to Use This Book

To develop a close and growing relationship with your partner you must know yourself and you must know your partner. The material in this book is designed to help you do just that.

Read carefully through each chapter and focus your thoughts on the attitudes, feelings and situations that are described and discussed, and which will affect the development of your relationship.

Most chapters contain exercises—questions to answer or statements to respond to—that will help you clarify your own attitudes, feelings and expectations. In chapters two, three, four six and ten, these exercises are part of the chapters themselves.

Chapters five, seven, eight, nine and eleven require that each partner respond to sets of statements about him or herself, and often about each other. These sets of statements are found in a convenient tear-out section at the end of the book. Each person may tear out a set of statements and respond to them independently, then discuss the responses with each other. Explanations of responses are also provided to help the discussions.

As you respond to the statements and discuss your responses, you will be learning about yourself and your partner, sharing yourself and building your relationship.

So simply start with chapter one and follow the carefully worded instructions that appear in **boldface type** as you come upon them.

Chapter 1

The Sacrament of Matrimony

The sacrament of matrimony is a truly beautiful event and recently we shared in just such an occasion. It made the meaning of marriage fresh again for us. The love that radiated from the bride and groom said it all, and the priest was tender and sensitive in reflecting his own happiness in witnessing the wedding.

In his homily he shared with the young couple what he considered to be the real message of Christian love—that it is lifelong, true and unselfish. He smiled and told them that there would be many times in the future when they might not like each other even though they were still in love. He pointed out that, in their humanity, feelings like anger, disgust and fear would make it hard for them to be in each other's presence.

At other times, one or the other might be frustrated because the spouse wouldn't or couldn't listen to a complaint, a hurt, or a plea for tenderness.

Their promise to love and honor each other, however, would be the bedrock of their relationship, the point from which they could overcome all obstacles. He said that two people love to the degree that they know each other, and that they honor to the degree that they are willing to accept each other. He said that the bad times would actually be opportunities for growth if they were open to one another at all times, and if each made an effort to understand what the other was experiencing.

It is exactly these commitments—to a marriage that is lifelong, true and unselfish—that help us understand the unique character of a Christian marriage.

We don't go before a civil authority to take our marriage vows. We go before God in the witness of the priest and/or minister. We are taking part in a sacrament, a symbol in which God is actually, actively present.

This sacrament of matrimony is a celebration—a celebration that expresses the realization that in marriage Christ touches the very core of our lives. It is a fundamental way to journey with Christ to the Father. But it is not just a sacrament at the time of the ceremony; it is a sacrament all through our lives.

This is the reason that the vow "to be true to you in good times and in bad, in sickness and in health and to love you and honor you all the days of my life," is not as crazy as some today would have us believe. In a time when more than a third of the couples who get married will not stay married, it is an achievable goal.

It is an achievable goal because a sacramental marriage is not based on any notion of law. It is based on love. Christ did not emphasize lists of laws to follow, rather he said to "love the Lord your God with all your strength . . . and . . . to love your neighbor as yourself" (Mk 12: 30-31). Christ's life was a message of love and his love for the couple entering marriage is a model for their love of each other.

St. Paul, in teaching Christ's message of love, said it was the greatest of all virtues and he offered a description that has never lost its accuracy. "Love is patient and kind; it is not jealous, or conceited or proud; love is not ill-mannered or selfish or irritable; love does not keep a record of wrongs, love is not happy with evil but is happy with the truth. Love never gives up; its faith, hope and patience never fail. Love is eternal" (1 Cor 13: 4-8).

A sacramental marriage, based on love, is not a contract between two people. It is a covenant. A contract is a legal arrangement which protects the rights of the individuals involved. It focuses on equity—that each partner get what he or she wants from the relationship, and that rights are protected. The contract can end when one of the partners breaks one of its conditions. In effect, a contract is a hedge against failure.

A covenant speaks to the relationship between God and his people. The church, through the Second Vatican Council, points out that, "As God of old made himself present to his people through a covenant of love and fidelity, so now the savior of men . . . comes into the lives of married Christians through the sacrament of matrimony."

When two people make their marriage vows, they are promising, as God promised in the covenant with his people, that the elements of love, forgiveness and faithfulness are always present. They are not hedging on their love or their promises. Christ taught that the Father was all-forgiving, merciful and that he would not abandon his people. So too in a sacramental marriage, the commitment is unconditional and open-ended. Change or the unforeseen does not end a covenant. The partners make their decisions based on love—they promise to give all freely and to expect nothing in return.

The "I will" spoken on the wedding day is only the beginning. Our behavior in married life tells if we have taken the commitment seriously. Our daily practice of love is what really matters, what will help the married relationship grow strong enough to sustain the ideals of the covenant, the ideals of the Christian sacramental marriage.

The story of a couple named Bernie and Kathy tells us of a marriage in which supporting behavior, this daily practice of love, was lacking. After eight years of marriage, they were totally frustrated. They were not angry with each other. But their marriage seemed dead.

Bernie explained: "When we were married, we intended to make this marriage last forever. We are both Catholic, come from stable families and we wanted to provide a good family life for our son. We tried to do the things that worked for our parents because we believed in a traditional marriage. I would be the breadwinner, and Kathy would be the mother and housewife.

"At first she agreed to this arrangement, but after our son John was born, things began to change. I would come home from work and expect Kathy to wait on me. I didn't help much around the house because that was Kathy's responsibility. Soon she began feeling more like a mistress and a maid than a wife and mother. She began asking me to listen to her frustrations, but I would always remind her that because she had nothing to worry about financially, she really had little to complain about. She felt that .there was absolutely no way for her to be a real human being in our marriage. She wanted to work outside the home in order to have some adult relationships. I guess I didn't mind because it got her off my back."

Kathy began looking for support and understanding through work away from home. "Work was a diversion for me," she said. "I liked what I was doing, and the people were kind and friendly. However, I soon began feeling guilty about leaving John with babysitters. My mother would never have done that. Although Bernie said he didn't mind my working, I could tell that he was less than happy with the arrangement. Before long we were coexisting in a marriage which was having less and less meaning for us. On the one hand, we wanted to stay together; on the other hand, our lack of mutual satisfaction kept driving us apart."

We can draw several clues from the example of Bernie and Kathy. Each had promised to love the other for life. However, their behavior did not fulfill the demands of that promise. They seemed to lose sight of the day-to-day, purely human aspect of a caring relationship. They treated their marriage like a contract. Each partner had prearranged specific responsibilities. When one or the other could not deal with the responsibilities, the relationship deteriorated. They were living by law rather than by love. They ignored feelings; they didn't listen to one another.

In our experience working as consultants to several Catholic marriage tribunals, we have found that marriage breaks down for several basic reasons. These include:

1. **Lack of self-understanding.** Oftentimes, a person reflects little self-understanding of the behavior that contributed to the breakdown of the marriage.

2. **Lack of understanding of the spouse.** At times, a person's own needs are so intense that an understanding of the spouse is seriously hampered.

3. **Inappropriate motivation for marriage.** So often a person entering marriage is motivated by reasons other than the responsible goals achievable in marriage. Some motives which are counterproductive include:

    a. marrying to escape an unsatisfactory home life,
    b. marrying because of social pressures,
    c. marrying to "reform" another person's behavior,
    d. marrying on the rebound,
    e. marrying to please the parents,
    f. marrying to spite the parents,

g. marrying because of pregnancy,

h. marrying with little knowledge of human sexuality,

i. marrying in spite of obvious interpersonal difficulties during the dating period.

4 **Poor models of marriage.** Some people get married with a negative attitude or impression of marriage. Perhaps their parents did not have a good marriage, or they have been exposed to the unhappy experiences of other couples. Usually they will have little insight into the tremendous potential for fulfillment and happiness in marriage.

5 **Poor communication techniques.** Some people get married without understanding how to communicate, how to relate to each other effectively. Because of a lack of understanding of self or of the spouse, and a lack of motivation, fear and anxiety develop in the relationship.

A caring or loving relationship is based on the awareness of needs. Each partner in a relationship must listen to the other and try to understand what the other is experiencing. Critical to this awareness is a commitment to the relationship. Only with commitment can the partners be real and open so that mistakes or problems do not lead to disaster.

Commitment alone, however, without awareness, is prone to failure. It becomes a hollow promise when one person in the relationship does not learn how to live lovingly for the partner. This kind of loving takes self-knowledge and knowledge of the partner—knowledge that develops in an open, accepting atmosphere.

This book is dedicated to helping you increase your awareness of yourself and your partner. It will do this by helping you and your partner understand your values and needs. It will also attempt to help you and your partner shape your behavior by being real, being understanding and being accepting. These conditions create the best climate for fulfilling the promises made during the wedding ceremony.

Chapter 2

Personality

We are going to begin with the most interesting person in the world—you!

Have you ever wondered, "Why do I do the things I do? How do people feel about me? What makes me tick?" What you are really asking is, "What's going on inside of me that makes me behave the way I do?"

Knowledge of yourself is very important in a marriage. It allows you to communicate with your partner, and with others, in a way that makes sense. Such understanding of yourself allows you to look at your behavior and see how it is affecting your marriage, and to make changes if necessary. The more you try to become the kind of person you know you ought to be as an effective husband or wife, the more comfortable you will feel. Equally important, you won't be afraid to let others see you as you really are in your relationships with them.

In order to answer some perplexing questions about yourself and your behavior, it is useful to learn some ideas about personality.

We all recognize that some people turn us on and others turn us off. Our judgments about personality tend to be fairly clear-cut—we see people as either pleasant or unpleasant.

If you think about people you know, those with pleasant personalities are easy to remember. You think readily of those who were friendly, trustworthy and dependable. A person I remember vividly was a high school teacher named Mr. Joyner. He was serious, but part of his seriousness came from his obvious concern for his students. I sensed this concern so strongly that I felt the need to produce in his class to the best of my ability.

As he saw his students grow and develop from his teaching, he drew great satisfaction. He never failed to compliment anyone who made a sincere effort. Even incorrect responses were handled as though they were steppingstones to success. I think the only time I saw him angry was when some of us laughed at a student who had made an obvious mistake. Mr. Joyner simply looked at us with a pained expression as though to say, "Don't be so unkind. Try to understand that this could happen to anyone, especially you."

On the other hand, you can remember people you have met who have left negative impressions because they were hostile, selfish or untrustworthy.

One man I knew like this was the manager of a lumberyard where I once worked. He was simply mean. He always berated people and was intolerant of mistakes. I remember in particular how badly he treated one worker who needed the job and dared not quit. The manager knew this, so he gave him the worst jobs, spoke to him vilely and offered no praise. As a result, no one liked the manager—he ate his lunch alone and went to and from work alone. His unpleasantness created a deep wedge between himself and others.

In order to explain such good and bad behaviors, specialists have tried to develop a theory of personality, hoping that such a theory would help people choose their life-styles. Defining behavior, though, is a vast and complicated problem that has yielded thousands of theories.

Most of these theories contain at least three common elements. They try to *describe behavior*, to *explain behavior* and to *predict behavior*.

If you stop to think about it, almost every choice you make involves some prediction. When you choose a marriage partner, you are predicting that this relationship is the best for you in satisfying the needs and sharing the values you bring to the marriage. So it is clear that you have to make judgments about personality even if you can't define it.

There are two personality theories that are especially useful for our discussion of behavior and how it relates to a successful marriage—the materialistic or physical theory and the Christian theory. Both represent explanations of human behavior that have great effect on life today.

Let's look at the theories and then relate their descriptions, explanations and predictions of behavior to the permanent, sacramental marriage.

The physical or materialistic theory states that humans have one basic drive, one motivation—physical pleasure. This pleasure is rooted in the body, is expressed through bodily action and, when satisfied, is momentarily at rest or ease. Sigmund Freud, a brilliant pioneer in the study of the human mind, calls this drive for physical satisfaction the libido. The libido sets its goal on any and all physical satisfaction, but essentially it is a drive for sexual fulfillment.

The relation of Freud's insights to modern life is apparent. Our society is pleasure-bent. The media seductively appeal to the drive for pleasure through the advertising for consumer goods.

In every respect the physical or materialistic theory of personality begins with a physical drive and ends with its satisfaction. And we can see that people actually do seek physical pleasure as an end in itself, at times disregarding any other possible explanation, description and prediction of behavior.

The second, or Christian theory, goes beyond the physical theory. It is directed to God and suggests that seeking truth and good is more appropriate than merely seeking pleasure.

If physical satisfaction is our only goal, then our behavior becomes a series of pleasure-seeking activities. If we formed a relationship with another person based strictly on the physical, the relationship could become jaded and other sex objects might become more appealing. The Christian theory of personality looks for more in a relationship than satisfying immediate physical needs.

The Christian theory is not against pleasure. It simply states that the drive for pleasure should be consistent with our nature; in other words, sex should be an expression of the *total* person. Bodily functions cannot be separated from feelings and reason. This theory speaks not only to physical pleasure but also to qualities such as goodness, truth, kindness, tenderness and love toward others.

In relating our theories to marriage, we can see that pursuit of pleasure emphasizes personal satisfaction even at the expense of the relationship. In the Christian context, physical pleasure emphasizes mutual satisfaction and thus supports the relationship. This mutual satisfaction requires more sensitive communciation, more intimate sharing, and therefore reinforces the commitments to permanency and fidelity. Pleasure becomes part of the total human encounter in the act of love.

Throughout this book you will have an opportunity to recognize how you make choices that represent one or the other of these ideas of behavior. Since our choices are based on our values and needs, let's begin by looking at our values.

Chapter 3

Values

One of the best ways to understand our behavior is to come to know our values and needs. At first this might sound complicated but, after a closer look, you will see that values and needs are rather easily understood.

First let's take a look at values. A value is a principle, standard, or quality considered worthwhile or desirable. The minute we use the word "considered," we are saying that a value rests in that part of our personality which we have called reason. Therefore, our values come about through some sort of reasoning process. We begin to say to ourselves, "I think that this principle or this quality or this person has a positive value for me." So at the present time much of our conscious behavior comes from the values we have developed over our lifetime. They direct our behavior to a large extent.

For example, if I am an actress and I value recognition, I might do some things which are illegal or immoral to gain recognition. I remember reading in the newspaper a while back about Arthur Bremer, the young man who allegedly shot George Wallace. Upon being apprehended, Arthur reportedly made the comment, "I will now go down in history for what I just did; I am no longer a nobody." He valued recognition to the point of breaking the law.

In almost any facet of living, we can find examples of values expressed through people's behavior. For example, we see joggers on paths and lanes throughout the U.S. When asked, "Why are you jogging?" people state different values. But there seem to be two basic values for jogging—maintaining good health and developing a good figure. Another good example of how a value directs a person's behavior can be seen in the politician who will sacrifice a career or family life to be elected.

Sometimes a value can bring difficulty to a person when that value is seen as contrary to our culture. I remember just such a man who was greatly misunderstood because he valued unselfish service to others. He seemed to spend all his time helping people without expecting pay. He was looked upon as odd, even crazy. In our culture, such selfless service is not usually held in high value. If we work, we expect pay. If we do something for someone, we expect a trade-off or some kind of help in the future.

But this man never sought pay or help from those whom he served. Actually, this value created problems in his own married life because his wife as well as others was perplexed by his behavior. Since he used this value also in being helpful to her, she could then tolerate it in his helping others. But it was still perplexing to her.

Not all husbands and wives can tolerate each other's values. We know of a couple who held such opposite values regarding money that their marriage was destroyed. Early in their married life they worked together running a little grocery in Chicago. He had a great talent for butchering, and during World War II, when meat was rationed, he knew how to carve every ounce of saleable meat from every carcass.

Their business prospered so rapidly that before long he was the owner of several grocery stores in the area. Since then he has become an industrial giant in a totally unrelated field. He had the genius of developing new talents in other areas as he saw changes taking place in American lifestyles. When asked why he left the grocery business, which he truly loved, he said that he valued money, and the luxury, renown and political power it could bring, much more. But this value came at great cost. He admits that he has no friends, has gone through several wives, and has no real relationship with his children.

A serious conflict arose in his first marriage because his wife held little value for money. When they were first married, she worked with him in their store. He needed her help and made sure that the hours she spent helping were rewarded by recognition, praise, and kindness. However, as the business grew, she became less and less important as he was able to hire more competent people. Eventually she was asked to leave the store altogether and manage their big, beautiful estate. At first that seemed wonderful, since she envisioned their having many pleasant hours together. Instead, as the business prospered and the demands on his time increased, she saw less and less of him. Any pressure she exerted to spend more time at home resulted in more absences. Finally, she posed the ultimate question: To choose between her and his business empire. They divorced.

In hindsight, the wife said she could see how his efforts to be kind to her were always centered around her usefulness to him in making money. Later she saw how he treated his employees the same way.

From this example we can see that people's different values can prevent them from living together comfortably. They will have difficulty in relating to each other because their behaviors are so different and because they cannot or will not try to understand each other's values. At best, they might form a truce through coming to know and respect each other's values without feeling threatened by them.

In marriage, therefore, the importance of knowing your own values and those of your partner is apparent. Knowing your values will help you recognize what behavior will be required and will help you decide what course of action to follow. Also, knowing your partner's values will help you recognize whether they coincide with or oppose your own, and will promote mutual understanding.

Values, then, can help to describe, explain and predict behavior. In the case of the successful executive, his value for money fits into this personality theory in the following way:

1. **Description of behavior:** His behavior was totally committed to making money. It tells *how* he used people, manipulated lives, and made deals—all to make money. When we describe behavior, we tell *how* a person acts in the pursuit of a value.

2. **Explanation of behavior:** The executive's behavior is explained by answering the question, "*Why* does he pursue the value of money?" He does so because it can bring him political power, renown, luxuries, and control of that part of the world in which he lives.

3. **Prediction of behavior:** The story of our executive's behavior points up the extreme positive value that he has for money. Therefore, it is fair to assume that he is going to continue his pursuit of it in the future with the same singleness.

This is not to say that valuing money is in itself good or bad. It simply states that anyone who hopes to relate with this man must recognize how his behavior is directed by his value of money. To expect any other behavior without a change of value on his part is unrealistic. His first wife could neither understand nor adapt to his pursuit of wealth. His second wife found it easy to understand his value because she shared it. Hence, she made no demands on him that didn't fit into his pattern of living. They didn't do much sharing, but they did use their wealth and power to establish social relationships and enjoy recreational activities.

Therefore, two people contemplating marriage must not only know their own values but also have some insight into how these values will affect their relationship. A marriage must be built on a firm set of values and convictions shared by both. These values give meaning and purpose to their life. Otherwise, conflicting values can create havoc in a relationship.

In this chapter we are going to talk about four values which we consider important in marriage because they promote interpersonal competency. They are:

1. **Recognition**
2. **Kindness**
3. **Independence**
4. **Responsibility**

Recognition

Taking each other for granted is a pitfall so common in marriage that it requires special emphasis. To understand it better, let's trace the usual pattern of how it comes about.

In the beginning a couple is drawn together through some kind of attraction. The man may be struck by her physical beauty; the woman by his virility. During the getting-acquainted period, both are highly sensitive to each other's feelings, moods, aspiration and goals. They discover qualities in each other that other people may not have appreciated; or they may deliberately ignore traits that others see as negative. In this sense love may indeed be blind.

Once they marry and settle into a routine, some of the novelty wears off, glowing praise takes a back seat and emotion loses its edge. Each person has duties to perform in making the marriage work, and they forget to give recognition. Actually they become more acute in picking up the partner's slack, and begin to inform each other of what is not being done well. She may no longer see him as her knight in shining armor, but as a tired husband in a battered Ford. He may return home and zero in on everything that's untidy before he even recognizes her presence. This mutual lack of recognition gives way to carping about deficiencies which were once overlooked.

Recognition helps counteract the tendency for spouses to take each other for granted. It emphasizes concern for the other and promotes sociability and friendship. Recognition means that the partners look for ways to give positive information to each other.

The marriage ceremony should be the starting point for greater recognition. Life together removes all facades—physical, emotional and mental. So as married life unfolds new and more profound discoveries should occur. Through mutual recognition the unique personalities of the partners will grow and develop.

We can see this growth and development when a couple gives public demonstration of their mutual recognition. At a recent social gathering we were impressed by a couple who were almost artistic in their expression of recognition. It didn't follow the usual pattern of husband and wife kidding each other. We have all been in situations where a husband might say, "My wife is a very careful shopper. She's careful not to look at prices, not to plan, and not to give a damn about saving money." Or a wife might say, "My husband is great around the house. He doesn't do much inside, but around the house he talks to neighbors, goes to the local beer joint, and hangs around with anyone who'll talk with him." By contrast, this couple always made positive statements about the partner like, "I feel pretty lucky because my wife is such a careful shopper. I see her carefully planning to buy the best bargains, even clipping coupons. I marvel at how she manages so well on so little money." At one point the wife said, "I don't have to worry about repairs around the house. He does his best to maintain everything in good running order, and he even tries to do things which I know are hard for him."

Apart from their own recognition of each other, this couple was attentive to what others had to say. They constantly tried to understand what was being said, and we can't recall that they ever made a negative judgment about other people's values. Recognition is so beneficial because it is positive. It says, "I want to listen to you; I want to understand you; I want to appreciate you; I want to allow you to be yourself in our relations."

We often see couples in counseling who don't value recognition, or can't express it positively. In general, when partners feel unrecognized, they are placed in a dilemma. They don't want to ask for recognition, and yet if they don't get it, they become angry and frustrated. As one wife said, "John has really changed since I married him. He used to notice everything about me, a new dress or a different hairdo. If I told him about some bit of praise from my employer, family, or friends, he enjoyed sharing such recognition. He admired me in front of others. Now after four years of marriage, I feel taken for granted. He never tells me I look nice anymore, keep a neat house, or that I'm a good wife and mother. A year ago I mentioned this to him, and his response was, 'You're just doing your job the way you're supposed to.' That's when we began going our separate ways. I simply stopped trying. I can't bear being taken for granted."

How can you tell if you have a high level of recognition for your partner? The best way is to examine the things you say and do for your partner. For example, a person who is sensitive to this value will make statements something like the following:

1. What a great person you are!
2. I appreciate how loving you are.
3. I can see how kindly you treat other people.
4. I like how you dress.
5. You're so thoughtful.
6. You're such an honest person.
7. You really work hard at everything.
8. You always try to do your best.
9. You always seem to know how to handle me.
10. So often you think of me before you think of yourself.
11. You never tear me down.
12. You always tell others what a great person you think I am.
13. You go out of your way for me.
14. You know how important my friends are to me.
15. You constantly remind me of your appreciation of my talents.

If you are inclined to make statements similar to these, you are telling your partner that you are aware of his or her positive attributes. To allow praiseworthy behavior to slip by unnoticed would do nothing for the relationship. We must constantly reinforce our partner's behavior and enhance closeness.

Kindness

As we have said, kindness requires an action on our part for our partner's benefit. For example, John may recognize Mary's wonderful qualities and praise her for her talents, good looks, and her goodness. He becomes sensitively kind to her when he does things for her. He knows that she loves roses, so he plants rose bushes for her. He knows she loves classical music, and buys her an album. John highly values doing things for Mary that he knows will please her.

Kindness prevents partners from measuring each other's contribution to the relationship. When partners are sensitively kind, they seldom "keep score" or make statements like, "You are not doing your part," or, "You do so little for me." Instead, kind spouses will say things like, "I appreciate your thoughtfulness," or, "You are something special. You are so kind to me," or, "You are really sensitive to my needs." Instead of measuring, kindness promotes positive action for each other's satisfaction.

Yet not all kindnesses are necessarily positive. Kindness can create problems in a marriage. Kindness is possessive when an act is done to control a person. A husband might buy a dream house miles away from everywhere so that his wife can't visit with her friends. A wife might buy gifts for her husband so that he can't complain about the money she spends on her wardrobe. Each does a "kind" act for the other in order to control the other's behavior.

Motivation helps us determine the direction of our kindness. If we are moved to help others for their good, we are sensitively kind. If we are moved to control others, we are possessively kind. Such "kindness" doesn't speak to the other person's needs or values. It doesn't allow the other person to be himself or herself.

Some examples of kindnesses are given below. Try to decide which ones are not possessive.

1. A wife knows her husband is facing an unusually difficult day at work. She decides to prepare his favorite meal, even though it will require extra work.

2. A husband wants to attend a ball game next week. This week he's going to bend over backwards to be kind to her in many little ways.

3. A husband knows his wife would like to buy a new dress for a special party, but that she won't spend the money unless he encourages her. He points out how well she handles their money and that a new dress will fit into their budget this month.

4. A husband wants to buy a new car, but his wife wants to buy new furniture. He very kindly helps her refinish the old sofa and chairs; later they buy a new car.

5. A daughter knows that her parents miss her very much. She tries to include them as much as she can in her personal and social life.

6. A son knows that his parents will always come to his rescue as long as he maintains contact with them. During hard times, he makes sure that he visits them often.

7. A wife notices that her husband is depressed. She concentrates on doing those things which she knows will help him work through his depression.

8. A husband becomes interested in a new hobby which has no appeal for the wife. She plans many mutually enjoyable social events which leave him little leisure time for his hobby.

9. A husband's work takes him away from home on Monday through Friday. He appreciates that his wife is homebound during that time. Although he would prefer staying home on weekends, he makes sure they have social activities outside the home.

10. A wife enjoys attending concerts and plays. The husband programs their social events on those nights when such cultural performances are not offered.

As you have probably guessed, the odd numbers are examples of sensitive kindness. The even numbers are examples of possessive kindness. While kindness creates a better relationship, possessive kindness prevents closeness and a good relationship. Remember, recognition tells our partner something positive about his or her behavior, while kindness requires some action on our part to nurture the partner's values and needs.

Independence

Independence allows each of the partners to be uniquely themselves in the relationship. Ideally, each should encourage the other to be real in showing their values and needs. This makes it easier for the partner to respond honestly without having to guess what is being communicated. Independence says, "I know you love me; I know you honor me; I know you wish to express your love and honor in a way which is most comfortable for you, and I know you would never want to force me to be something I am not." The good of our partner motivates this kind of independence. It is centered on the other.

Spouses must be aware that negative feelings generated from the expression of one-sided independence can be frightening. For example, if one partner has failed to express recognition and kindness to the other, independence can be seen as a barrier to their relationship. A husband might say to his wife, "I'm just not given to praising others. You know I work hard for you, and that's how I show my kindness. I want to be free to do things my way. Just keep in mind that that's the way I am." This kind of independence strikes terror into a partner's heart. It makes the partner feel isolated in the relationship because there is no positive feedback from such behavior. It lacks mutuality.

Let's go over the following illustrations and try to distinguish which ones reflect mutual independence:

1. A husband insists that it is his right to go bowling with the boys every Tuesday night because it has always been part of his lifestyle, even before marriage.

2. A wife is an antique expert. Occasionally this takes her out of the home, but the husband encourages her in this hobby because it means so much to her.

3. A wife insists on working outside the home. This makes her husband angry since they don't need the money.

4. A husband feels compelled to make weekly visits to his mother who is in a nursing home. The wife recognizes his need and encourages his expression of concern for his mother.

5. A wife feels a need to render services to her church. She does so in spite of her husband's objections that her primary responsibilities at home are not being taken care of.

6. A husband frequently enjoys having his co-workers in for dinner. Even though it creates a great deal of extra

work for her, his wife encourages him to feel free to do so.

7. A husband finds great pleasure in telling dirty jokes. He also knows that his wife feels uncomfortable when he tells them, but he does so anyhow.

8. For his next vacation a husband would like to visit some of his old school buddies. His wife has no particular desire to do anything special, so she encourages him to plan the kind of vacation he would like.

9. A husband is a clotheshorse. Since he earns the money, he feels he should be able to dress in style.

10. A wife feels compelled to get involved in politics. Her husband is not politically inclined, but still encourages his wife to fulfill her political commitments.

The even-numbered examples reflect mutual independence. The odd-numbered ones reflect a kind of isolated independence which ignores the binding force of the relationship. Through awareness of each other's values and needs, the partners allow each other to be themselves in activities which promote their feelings of well-being. This doesn't mean that either has the right to do whatever he or she pleases, but instead each makes an effort to be open to the uniqueness of the other. Each allows the other the freedom to pursue certain interests. Neither becomes threatened by such activity, but instead encourages the partner to feel free to be herself or himself in the activity.

Responsibility

In part, responsibility means the fulfillment of obligations in a relationship or lifestyle. A noted psychologist once wrote that most negative feelings begin when we shirk our responsibilities. When we evade our duty, it makes us feel bad. We become angry with ourselves, try to blame others, or, in general, feel anxious. It would seem as though we simply can't escape the ill effects of irresponsibility.

Our responsibility in marriage is to foster a more effective relationship between each other. It is one thing to say "I love you," it is another to express this love through our behavior. Such behavior will require constant vigilance to do those things which will promote the well-being of our partner. When we turn away from this responsibility, the relationship will tend to flounder or fall apart. The promises made in the sacrament of matrimony will be fulfilled only to the extent that each partner carries out his or her mutual responsibilities to develop a better relationship.

The following examples deal with various decisions made in a relationship. Decide which are responsible or irresponsible.

1. A husband has been offered a promotion which would require moving to another city. He is very close to his mother and knows she doesn't want them to leave. He passes up the promotion.

2. A wife goes on a clothes-buying spree. Usually she is quite frugal with their money, but because of this one splurge, the husband decides to handle the money.

3. A couple is finding it difficult to manage on the husband's earnings and have recently had serious financial difficulty. The wife wants to work to clear up the debts, but the husband refuses because of what his family might say.

4. A couple feels the need to be free of their children once in a while. They discover a club with social activities that both enjoy. They join.

5. A husband dislikes his work and comes home frustrated, angry, and short-tempered. His family finds this condition intolerable, but he refuses to seek work elsewhere.

6. A neighbor close by is very lonely. She is shy and finds it difficult to reach out to others. A married couple tries to draw her out by being kind and doing things for her.

7. A wife would like to take some adult education courses for personal enrichment. The husband thinks this is a waste of time and money. He makes her feel guilty, so she decides not to take the courses.

8. A husband decides to join his wife in her churchgoing activities. This gives her great joy.

9. A husband and wife decide that their friends are inclined to drink too much. Neither particularly cares for liquor, so they seek out new friends.

10. Both husband and wife work outside the home. Each feels that the household chores should be done without measuring.

Examples one, two, three, five, and seven deal with irresponsible decisions. Four, six, eight, nine, and ten reflect responsible decisions.

In reviewing all four values, remember that recognition, kindness, mutual independence, and responsibility are all values that help build a better relationship between two people. When each partner acts upon these values, they create an atmosphere of openness and freedom to be oneself in the relationship. These values reduce fear. They reduce the threat and feeling of vulnerability that come from taking risks with the partner. As we said earlier, the relationship is founded on the promise to love and honor one another. This is the continuing process of love freely given without measure—without selfishness.

Permanency in marriage requires that a couple constantly strive to facilitate their ability to relate well to each other, to grow and develop. In part, this means that they concentrate on the values we have discussed.

Chapter 4

Needs

Values are reflected in the judgments we make, and thus are associated with the reasoning area of our personality. From the standpoint of reason, then, values give direction to our behavior.

Another part of our personality deals with what we call needs.

Hunger is a need. When I am hungry, I feel the physical pangs which tell or "drive" me to eat. So in technical terms we can say that needs produce drives that are associated with our physical or emotional being.

Emotionally I might feel the need for affection. This need creates a drive which seeks satisfaction by obtaining affection from another person. Actually this emotional drive can be as strong as a physical drive, such as the one for food, and can sometimes even create what feels like a physical drive.

Overeating is an example. It is usually considered to be more of an emotional than a physical problem. Yet people who overeat say they feel hungry even though they know they have consumed enough food to meet their physical needs.

There are some interesting aspects about needs. We can feel a need even though we can't give a good reason for its existence. I remember a man once saying that there were times when he experienced the need to get drunk. When asked why and how the conditions existed he couldn't give a reason. Another interesting aspect about needs is that we become frustrated if we experience a need and don't satisfy it. Our frustration keeps building as the need remains unsatisfied until finally we lash out at some person or thing.

Let's explore the case of Tom and Sally to see how unfulfilled needs work. Their complaint was similar to that of other couples: "My needs are not being satisfied in this marriage." Tom was 21 and Sally was 19 when they were married six years ago. They had known each other for most of their lives. After graduation from college, Tom became a management trainee for a large retail chain, and Sally was employed as a social worker. They bought a dream home, each had a car, and were even able to save some money. About two years ago they realized that certain aspects of their behavior were causing them problems. Although Tom had progressed fairly well in his work, he began pushing hard for some changes in their lifestyle. Becoming bored with both his work and the routine of their marriage, he felt he needed a change. Sally became concerned about his behavior because he wasn't following the pattern of a successful young businessman. His appearance became sloppy, he was spending too many nights out with the boys, and he stopped going to church: she was embarrassed because people began talking. She needed order in her life and became dissatisfied because Tom was causing disorder. His need for change and her need for order were in conflict. With insight, they were amazed at how little they really knew each other. They also learned how difficult it would be for them to satisfy each other's needs. And their continuing frustration made life miserable. Both said that if they had been aware of all this when dating, their marriage might never have taken place.

The case of Tom and Sally suggests how important it is to learn all we can about needs and how they fit into the marriage relationship. A good starting point is to understand how a need develops. Most researchers agree that needs arise out of early parent-child relationships and the kind of learning climate that parents create. For instance, if parents are accepting, encouraging, and responsive to their children's actions early in life, then their children will develop "good" habits which will prove to be productive. But if early parent-child relationships are faulty, then some of these early traits could develop into habits which might prove to be disruptive.

It might be helpful here to trace the development of a need through the example of Mr. Jones and his son Johnny. Mr. Jones recognized his son's special talents very early. He felt that his responsibility as a father was to provide the best conditions possible for Johnny to develop these talents. As young Johnny explored new and different toys, situations, and people, Mr. Jones carefully supported his son in these activities by allowing Johnny to experience both success and failure. This encouraged the boy to take more and more risks, to try new and different things, and to feel secure in his father's support. Mr. Jones stimulated Johnny's natural curiosity; the only restraint he placed on his own son was to make sure that Johnny didn't hurt himself or others in the learning process.

As a result, Johnny developed some traits that are basic to the need to achieve. He became innovative, a moderate risk-taker, unafraid to make mistakes, and developed the courage of his convictions. Through his experiences, little Johnny also learned to appreciate people, to recognize the importance of relationships, and to reach out to others.

It is easy to see how Johnny's positive development resulted in helpful lifelong traits. However, another example can illustrate what happens in a learning situation less favorable than Johnny's. Mr. Smith never seemed to have time to spend with his son Eddie. When Eddie looked to his father for support and encouragement, it was never there. Instead, his father became angry and literally pushed the boy aside. Eddie began feeling that being passive and taking no risks was the safest course of action. Even worse, he began thinking that there was something wrong with himself. In adulthood, his fears and attitudes disrupted his attempts at relating with people.

The examples of Johnny and Eddie show how our learned needs can help or hinder our relations with others. In the case of Johnny we saw that positive experiences early in life tended to develop needs which helped build harmonious human relationships. In Eddy's case we saw that other early learned needs became habits which disrupted interpersonal relationships, created a poor self-image, and caused tension.

Another way to learn about needs is to come to recognize them in ourselves and others. We can do so by first learning what is meant by positive and negative needs. Second, we can look for behavior that helps us to identify needs. Below is a list of positive and negative needs as they function in our relations with others.

I. POSITIVE NEEDS
A. WARM NEEDS: (warm needs bring people together through positive feelings).
1. The need to GIVE affection
2. The need to RECEIVE affection
3. The need for COMPANIONSHIP
4. The need to SHARE warmth through sexual activity

B. NEEDS FOR EFFECTIVE COMMUNICATION: (these needs bring people together through understanding).
5. The need to be OPEN to messages from others
6. The need to UNDERSTAND the messages.

II. NEGATIVE NEEDS: (these needs disrupt our relations with others because they tend to keep people apart).
1. The need to be AGGRESSIVE
2. The need for one person to DOMINATE another
3. The need to TEAR oneself down

In order to understand these positive and negative needs we will describe each one. Included in the description are some statements which reflect the behavior that could follow from such needs.

POSITIVE NEEDS

The Need to Give Affection

The need to be affectionate is a GIVING need on our part which can be shown in many ways. We see it in the mother giving affection to her newborn child, or in the lover reaching out to the beloved. As a general rule, this need to be affectionate is a learned drive stemming from experiences in childhood through the giving and receiving of affection between parent and child. As adults, and particularly as engaged or married couples, the need to give affection might be shown in the following statements or actions:

1. I love to touch my partner.

2. I have a strong need to be warm to my partner.

3. I get a great deal of satisfaction in speaking lovingly to my partner.

4. I feel very satisfied when I am in my partner's presence.

5. I often daydream about showering attention upon my partner.

Such statements or actions suggest that giving affection is an important need for a person. Of course, this is all very productive for effective relations with others if the need can be expressed in behavior that benefits the partnership.

The Need to Receive Affection

The reciprocal of the need to give affection is the need to RECEIVE affection. In an extreme form, this need can be seen by a person pretending to be sick just to be treated with kindness. A stereotype might be the mother, facing the loss of an only son in marriage, who feigns illness so that she will not lose her only source of affection. In even more extreme situations, we hear people in emergencies crying out, "Oh, God, help me!" or "Oh, mother, where are you?" These are calls for someone to help them in time of need. In a less dramatic situation, it is not unusual for a person to say, "Gee, I wish I had someone to love me."

Sometimes a person may have no need for affection, and the person offering the affection sees this as rejection. The following dialogue is an example of a partner needing to give affection, but the other with no need to receive it. A husband and wife are in bed and their exchange goes something like this:

Husband: "Gosh, it's good being in bed together."

Wife: "Well, I've had a rough day and I'm really tired."

Husband: "Roll over and let me hold you."

Wife: "We both have very busy days tomorrow. If we start something, it's going to take away from our sleeping."

Husband: "I would like to make love."

Wife: "I don't have the energy or desire. Let's just go to sleep. I sometimes think you are too affectionate."

Another example might be a person needing to receive affection and expressing it through actions. A wife has been home all day and is eagerly awaiting her husband's return from work. She is wearing a new dress, has had her hair done, has mixed his favorite drink, and turned on soft music. The husband arrives home, looks at her, looks around, and asks, "What's the big occasion? I hope there's nothing on tonight because all I want to do is watch TV and relax."

In this example, the wife had the need to receive affection but the husband no need to give it. These real-life situations show how easy it is to miss each other's signals or cues if we are not sensitive or "in tune."

The need to receive affection is sometimes heard in the following expressions:

1. I wish my partner showed me more affection.

2. I wish my partner would show me more attention in time of need.

3. I wish my partner would demonstrate more care for me.

4. I often daydream about my partner showering me with affection.

5. I wish my partner would say "I love you" outside of the bedroom.

The Need for Companionship

The third warm need might be called the need for friendship. Although there seems to be no precise definition for friendship, all of us seem to know when we have a friend. Friends are generally supportive. They will come to us in time of need, as we would go to them. Friendships set up human contacts involving common interests which we may enjoy without fear of judgment, contradiction, or evaluation. Such a need is apparent by the large number of social clubs, some of which are even called fraternities or sororities. The common element of these associations is that people gather together in a spirit of goodness and friendship because they want to be with each other.

It is self-evident that husband and wife should be very close friends. They should enjoy each other's company, share a number of mutual interests, and find it profitable to "waste time together." If this need to be together does not exist in the marriage, then companionship might be sought elsewhere. I once knew a husband whose need for companionship was so great that it brought his marriage almost to divorce. His friends were numerous, and he enjoyed being with them more than being with his wife. He would volunteer for committee work, willingly performing tasks left undone by others. His wife saw his hyper-activity as a threat to their marriage. She began feeling that his friends were more important to him than she was. He gained insight only after she threatened divorce and they sought counseling. From this we can see that companionship between husband and wife must have first priority, and that outside social activities are best kept secondary to the marriage relationship.

Comments such as the following reflect the general need for companionship:

1. I need personal contact with friendly people.
2. I need the give-and-take of friendly relationships.
3. I miss not being around my friends.
4. I become very nervous when I know I can't contact my friends.
5. I become very depressed when I am slighted by a friend.

The Need to Share Warmth Through Sexual Activity

The fourth warm need might be called a sexual need. Unlike the first three, satisfying this need requires actual physical contact with a person of the opposite sex. It becomes a mutual experience in which both actively participate in a physical expression.

At this point it is necessary to distinguish between sex and sexuality. Sex has to do with those physical characteristics which make a person male or female. On the other hand, sexuality encompasses the total being and includes not only the physical expression but also the emotional, intellectual, and social ways of being a mature, fulfilled man or woman.

In this section we are speaking strictly of the need to fulfill the physical sex drive. Men and women experience this drive when they seek contact through sexual intercourse. Some of the statements that indicate the need to fulfill this drive include:

1. I often feel a strong urge to caress my spouse.
2. I feel a strong need to experience sexual relations with my spouse.
3. I feel a strong need to be responsive to my spouse's sexual advances.
4. I often fantasize about having sexual intercourse with my spouse.
5. I often feel a strong urge to make sexual advances to my spouse.

In a later chapter we will expand on the difference between sex and sexuality and how these differences fit into the two personality theories we are using. But for now we will continue to describe the other needs listed in our outline.

While the four needs just discussed (Give Affection, Receive Affection, Companionship, Heterosexual Experiences) express what we called warm needs, there is another set of positive needs that involve communication with others.

The Need to Be Open to Messages from Others

This need can be divided into two separate steps necessary for communication. The first is the need to be OPEN to messages from others and the second is the need to UNDERSTAND what the messages are saying.

The first step means that when we allow someone to send us a message, we must listen and be open to it without accepting or rejecting it. It is as though we defer or set aside whatever we have to say in favor of being open to what the other person is saying. This is so important, that if openness isn't present, then messages never get through to us. When we come across as being stubborn or as having all the answers, we simply block out messages. It is important to make a distinction here and not confuse being open to messages with agreeing to messages. Agreeing or disagreeing involves making a judgment—a kind of filtering process. But when we listen to understand, we are not necessarily accepting or rejecting.

The need to be OPEN to what others are saying can be expressed by such statements:

1. I need to listen to what my partner says.
2. I need to be open to suggestions from others, especially my partner's.
3. I need to seek as much information as possible before making a decision.
4. I need to curb my own prejudices in order not to block out information being given me.
5. I need to have others share in the decision-making process.

The Need to Understand What the Messages Are Saying

The first step is to be OPEN to the message, and the second is to try to UNDERSTAND what the person is saying. It is important that we keep this point in mind, otherwise we try to understand the message in terms of what it means to us. Our frame of reference or viewpoint might be different from the person speaking, and if we don't try to keep the message in his or her context, we could easily distort it.

Following are statements which reflect a need to UNDERSTAND what a person is saying:

1. I have a need to understand people.
2. I have a need to know what it is like for someone to relate to me.
3. I have a need to understand the motives of others (*why* people do things rather than *what* they do).

4. I have a need to help people express what's on their minds.

5. I have a need to understand rather than make value judgments.

A good illustration of a failure in communications might be a father and son. Each feels a deep need to communicate with the other and tries to do so by sending messages from their respective points of view. For example, let's say the father is very anxious for his son to go to college. The father is a self-made man who very early in life worked himself into a responsible position with a large corporation. He realizes that with a better education he could have advanced further. Even though less capable than himself, many of his associates were promoted because the company felt that the better educated had more potential.

In the meantime, the son enjoyed the fruits of his father's labors and witnessed what an uneducated man could achieve. Also he noticed that a better education didn't always guarantee a higher position.

So father and son discussed the young man's future, and the father said something like this: "Son, I don't want you to go through life without an education and have to struggle for promotions as I've had to. We have the money now to send you to the best schools, and you have the talent to make it. So I want you to seriously consider going to college; you can study whatever you want, but I do want you to get a degree."

Now the son was not open to this message, and replied, "Dad, I see no real reason to go to school. You've done all right, and that's good enough for me. Right after high school, I want to go to work, start at the bottom, and work myself up the way you did." In effect, the son is saying, "Dad, I want to be just like you. You did it the hard way, so I want to do it the hard way. You've enjoyed a good life; therefore, I can enjoy a good life, too." The son is really trying to communicate this message to his father, just as the father is trying to communicate his message to the son. Each has a need to communicate, but the two basic factors essential for true communication are not present. The first factor is that neither is completely open to what the other is saying; second, neither really understands what the other is really trying to say.

You might ask, "Well, what can they do? Who is to win, and who is to lose?" It is not a question of winning or losing, but a question of how they can learn and develop a process to resolve this kind of deadlock through openness and understanding.

NEGATIVE NEEDS

The Need to Be Aggressive

In addition to the positive needs which we have discussed, there are negative needs which arise, in part, from faulty examples in early life. Perhaps the most devastating, counterproductive need that we tend to develop through childhood is the need to be AGGRESSIVE, usually the result of some kind of frustration.

By frustration we mean a situation created when a barrier is placed between us and a goal. We see this acted out in infancy when a baby gets red-faced, screams, and kicks when searching for a nipple out of reach. In baby language, that is aggression. Then we see the child in the terrible two's beginning to thrash about when frustrated. A classic example is temper tantrums. The child learns early that by throwing a tantrum it can persuade an insecure mother to satisfy its every desire. So, in these childhood experiences the need to be aggressive begins to develop.

If we define aggression as an act committed to hurt someone, then it is easy to see that an aggressive act works against relating well with others. Since it is a common drive resulting from frustration, and since it divides us, we would profit from managing aggression in the most productive way possible. When we are aggressive with our partner, it causes him or her to be defensive, frightened, threatened and unable to continue an effective I-Thou relationship. Perhaps scripture teaches us, in part, to turn the other cheek because aggression really only causes more aggression.

The following statements are indicative of the need to be aggressive:

1. I have a need to argue for the sake of argument.
2. I have a need to attack contrary points of view.
3. I have a need to provoke confrontations.
4. I have a need to do battle at the slightest frustration.
5. I need the satisfaction of overwhelming others.

The Need for One Person to Dominate Another

Another negative need is to be DOMINANT. When exercised, it prevents people from expressing themselves naturally. Like all other needs, it begins with childhood experiences. It might start with sibling rivalry. Through intense competition with brothers and sisters we learn that dominance allows us to control a situation for personal gain. This need to control can be felt in other situations. In a social setting, it might surface as the need to control the discussion. In a work situation, it can come across as the need to make a fellow worker subservient.

The point is that a need to dominate comes across as a strong drive to control a situation to one's own advantage. For obvious reasons, this works against relating well with others. First of all, it creates subservience or anger in another, depending on how well the controlled person can cope.

But probably the most significant negative aspect of dominance is that it does not allow the other people to be themselves. Without freedom of self-expression, a person is denied the opportunity to choose growth-promoting experiences. There is no give-and-take and very little creative learning, because the dominated person is prevented from participating in the decision-making process in a relationship.

Here are five statements that help us understand the need to dominate:

1. I need to control other people.
2. I need to have the final say in any matter.
3. I have the need to make sure that my ideas prevail in an argument.
4. I have the need to control discussions.
5. I have the need to be "center stage" in a social gathering.

The Need to Tear Oneself Down

Again, like the other ones, this need begins early in life when we are exposed to partial rejection. As children, we may have tried to accomplish something, but the result of our effort was greeted with, "Well, that's all right, *but* . . . ." Then we feel deflated because we are not encouraged to take risks, to seek fulfillment, to develop any sense of optimism, or to experience a feeling of total worth. Making little of oneself becomes a negative force between people because it tends to say, "You don't want to relate with me because I can't do anything very well." The person who belittles himself will keep others at a distance for fear that closeness will result in some negative judgment like, "You're all right, but . . . ." Obviously, if we cannot get close to a person, the possibilities of a rewarding relationship are severely crippled.

In a way, tearing ourselves down tends to sap our energies. There is such a fear of failure and rejection that we waste a great deal of energy worrying about what we ought not to do. Hence, we don't take risks because we think we are going to fail anyway. It becomes a self-fulfilling prophecy of defeat.

The following comments tell us something about the need to belittle ourselves:

1. I need to hold back because of my fear of failing.
2. I need to play down compliments paid me.
3. I need to play down what few talents I have.
4. I need to be led because of my poor leadership qualities.
5. I need to be free of taking risks, such as being responsible for almost anything.

In reviewing, it can be easily seen that values and needs are important factors in our search for rewarding relationships. Remember, values are thinking functions. Needs are usually felt as impulses or drives requiring some sort of action to satisfy them. Stated simply, we think our values, but we feel our needs. Values and needs, then, give shape to our behavior.

Being our true selves or being real in expressing our values and needs encourages others to be genuine also.

Chapter 5

Being Real

In general older personality theories emphasized pessimistic factors and negative goals. In contrast, modern theorists stress optimistic factors and positive goals. They state that if the right conditions exist between two people, they can be of great help to one another. These "right" conditions are fairly simple and can be learned by almost any two people willing to make the effort.

Three of these conditions are:

1. The two people must be real to each other.
2. They must try to understand what it is like to be the other person.
3. They must care for each other in such a way that neither one feels trapped by this caring.

In technical terms we call these three conditions being *genuine*, being *accurately empathetic*, and being *nonpossessively warm*. If one of the conditions is missing, the growth of the relationship will be affected.

A person who profoundly influenced me by being genuine, understanding, and caring, was Father Zak. I met him when I was an eighth-grader at St. Joan of Arc School. He was assigned to our parish temporarily because our own pastor was ill. The year was 1935 when the country was in a severe depression, and our parish was very poor and much in debt. The main industry in town had folded in 1929, and the workers were unable to find employment. As I recall, most of the families were on welfare. Our little parish numbered about 100 families. Since no one could contribute more than a coin or two in support of the church, our collections were scanty. The pastor was poor as well and visited his parishioners by bicycle.

Father Zak maintained the dignity of his priesthood and at the same time showed the simplicity of a man who was truly human. He understood poverty and shared this understanding with his parishioners. His care extended to all. He learned the name of each member of his parish, and he knew who was hurting and whose needs were the most pressing. I remember that his example inspired others to be real, to be understanding, and to be caring. Following his lead, the men in the parish soon got together to provide labor for those needing help, and the women shared their domestic talents in caring for those families in distress. On the day of his departure, so many people came to his last Mass that it had to be held outdoors. There were few dry eyes. As a teenager I couldn't realize or identify his wonderful attributes, but I somehow knew he was a truly great human being.

I also recall other people who weren't so real and how it affected our relationships. I remember a friend's mother who was very kind to her children when other adults were around. She would speak sweetly to them and tend to their every need. But once the adult left, she became harsh and intolerant. I felt very wary and cautious with her. I couldn't be real. In general, I have come to believe that realness in a person generates realness in others, but non-genuineness makes others defensive or puts them on their guard.

In marriage this element of realness is the foundation for a caring and understanding relationship. Unrealness erodes the foundation, and the relationship becomes shaky. In my mind, the importance of genuineness in a marriage can't be exaggerated—it is absolutely essential if two people are to relate freely with each other. Countless couples have come to my office for marriage counseling, and almost always one partner accuses the other of being non-genuine. I recall one couple in particular, in which the wife accused the husband of being non-genuine. Her story went something like this:

"Jim and I have been married for 20 years. During our courtship he was the most tender, kind, and caring man that I had ever met. It seemed as though I was more important to him than any other person or relationship—even his profession. At that time he was just beginning his law practice and was immediately successful. In spite of his success, he still had a great deal of time to spend with me, and we enjoyed a wonderful courtship. I remember that he said he didn't live to practice law; he practiced law in order to live. That impressed me. His main goal in life was to be a good husband and father, and said nothing would stand in his way.

"We had three children within the first five years of marriage. I began noticing that Jim didn't care much about helping me with the children. His clients began taking more and more of his time. Finally when I became so overwhelmed with caring for the children, I approached Jim about the statements he made during our courtship. He said that at that time he didn't realize how much more demanding his practice would be, but if I really felt that way, then he would try to help out. That was immediately forgotten the next day. Then other situations began cropping up where Jim would say things to satisfy me but would never act on his word. Even his kindness and sensitiveness began slipping to the point where he seemed to just go through the motions with no meaning. So after 20 years I've reached the point of wondering who this man is I've married. He seems *unreal!* I don't know who the real Jim is anymore, what the real Jim wants, or where our marriage is headed. The children are all teenagers now, and they've pretty much written him off. It isn't that he hasn't provided well for us . . . but I must add that he provides even better for himself. Ironically, when we go to the club together, he puts on a great show for the other members. He fawns over me, is very caring of the children, and smiles benignly at his wonderful family. He does this very successfully because so many of the club members have said to me, 'My, what a fine husband and father Jim is.' I guess it's at those times that I really want to stand up and scream, 'You don't know the real Jim.' "

This situation is sad because initially their marriage showed so much promise. It shows what lack of genuineness can do to what could have been a satisfying marital relationship.

It's easier to talk about genuineness than it is to practice it in our daily lives, because sometimes people make it hard for us to be genuine. It's as though they erect barriers which keep us from being our true selves when we do really want to be. That's why it can be very helpful to recognize that there seem to be some common barriers between men and women which prevent each other from being real.

Couples who participate in our marriage preparation courses try to deal with these barriers by surfacing them. We will pass on the results of an exercise which they have found very informative and helpful.

When we discuss being real, the couples brainstorm about sex differences which seem to create barriers to genuineness. In other words, the women discuss what there is about men that makes it difficult for women to be genuine, and the men go through the same process. The results of these brainstorming exercises are remarkable in their consistency. Disregarding age or geographic location, almost all groups say the same thing. Specifically, women cite the following attributes about men that make it difficult for women to be real:

1.   Men get angry too quickly.
2.   Men's egos are so fragile.
3.   Men hide their emotions.
4.   Men try to be too logical.
5.   Men confuse affection with sex.
6.   Men want to dominate.
7.   Men give women little credit for having any brains.
8.   Men won't allow women the free expression of feelings.
9.   Men won't communicate; they pout.
10.   Men are jealous of the friendships that women have.

Now many other traits are brought up as well, but these ten seem to be the most frequently voiced. Since they surface almost every time in every workshop, it would seem safe to say that men must keep these ten characteristics in mind and be aware of any effect these masculine characteristics might have on their wives.

Men bring up the following ten barriers that women create that keep the men from being real:

1. Women talk too much.

2. Women can't make decisions very easily.

3. Women use tears to control men.

4. Women use sex as a weapon.

5. Women want independence, but when they get into trouble, they want the men to rescue them.

6. Women want to keep up with the Joneses.

7. Women are inconsistent; they say one thing but mean another.

8. Women's feelings are too easily hurt.

9. Women are too sensitive and emotional.

10. Women are jealous of male activities, such as hunting, fishing, and sports.

Particularly in the marriage relationship both men and women must be aware of the behaviors which make it difficult for the partner to be real. These lists are in no way indicative of how all men or how all women behave, but it is useful to know that many couples have cited these traits as creating problems.

In order to help you and your partner better understand the function of genuineness in your relationship, we have included a series of statements for you to respond to. The format is similar to that of the questionnaires presented in Chapter 3 on Values. Turn to pages 115-120 for directions and worksheets on "Being Real."

Chapter 6

Defense Mechanisms

When we cannot be genuine in a relationship, it is usually because we feel threatened. A threat makes us defensive or frightened and it is difficult to be real. One way to protect ourselves is to create a barrier between us and the threat. We call this barrier a defense mechanism.

For example. Let's suppose a young man falls in love with a beautiful young woman. This young woman is extremely popular and is pursued by many boyfriends who take her to the finest places. She also has the reputation of being very choosey, and sometimes is even quite cruel to those courting her. She seems to enjoy having a great number of boys chasing her—the more the better.

This young man who is so attracted to her is very sensitive, shy, and lacking in self-confidence. He would dearly love to ask her to be his steady girlfriend, but feels threatened by what he has heard. He fears he might be hurt by her rejection, because many others have. Rather than take the risk, he begins making excuses so as to protect his ego. That's how a defense mechanism works. When the threat is too great, we spontaneously and unconsciously throw up barriers to avoid hurt or pain.

Defensiveness can be very much like a reflex act. If we touch a hot stove, we instantly pull back our hand. We do not stop and think, nor do we direct our actions. They just happen. The ego defense mechanism works exactly the same way. When our ego is

65

threatened, we respond to the situation in a spontaneous, unconscious way.

Let's say that your fiancee tells you that she thinks you are very inconsiderate in talking about her family. You are offended and immediately respond that that isn't true. You are in effect only denying the accusation and not dealing with the fact of it.

In a significant relationship like marriage, it is important to recognize not only your own defensiveness but also that of your partner, because one of you may be causing the other to feel threatened. If the one causing the threat is able to recognize it, then the situation can be remedied, but if the partner who is the source of the threat cannot see it, then defensiveness just grows and grows until the situation becomes unbearable.

Perhaps we can see what can happen when defensiveness is not worked through. Joe Smith has the habit of comparing his wife Polly to his mother. No matter what Polly does, she always suffers by comparison. Her ego is threatened because she feels that she is not as competent as her mother-in-law. Because she fears the loss of Joe's love, she becomes very defensive whenever Mrs. Smith is present. If this defensiveness continues to grow, it could threaten the relationship with her husband.

Now let us look at five possible ways that Polly might respond defensively to this situation:

1. **Emotional Insulation:** One of Polly's defensive responses might be to protect her ego by withdrawing into an emotional cocoon so that feelings cannot get in or out. She becomes very formal with Mrs. Smith, never daring to show her true feelings or perhaps any feelings at all. For example, Polly doesn't risk showing anger because that might displease Joe. If she tries to be like her mother-in-law, she feels she would still suffer by comparison in Joe's eyes. So Polly invests no part of herself in relating with Joe or his mother by pulling back into emotional passivity.

2. **Rationalization:** Polly might handle her sense of failure by making excuses. She could say that it's perfectly normal for a young husband to think of his mother in such positive terms. Polly might say something like, "Joe certainly lived with his own mother longer than he has with me. I know he loves me in a very

special way even though he tends to be more expressive to his mother than he is to me." Polly doesn't compete with her mother-in-law because to do so would be too threatening and so she must make excuses for not competing.

3. **Projection:** Polly might respond to the threat she is experiencing by blaming her fears on either Joe or his mother, or both. She might say, "I feel very nervous around my mother-in-law because she is over-critical and doesn't like me," when, in fact, Mrs. Smith has never really been over-critical or shown dislike for Polly. Or Polly might say, "His mother is so demanding of him that Joe is too weak to stand up to her and tell her what a great wife I really am." In this way Polly defends herself against the fear of failure by blaming someone else. This kind of defense mechanism is like rationalization, but takes it one step further—it casts blame upon others.

4. **Displacement:** A fourth way that Polly might defend her ego is to lash out at someone or something other than Joe and his mother. For example, the paperboy might irritate her by ringing the bell too long or too insistently, and she discharges her pent-up feelings by berating him. Actually, the real source of her anger was Joe's comment when he left for work, "I hope you won't embarrass me by not having the house cleaned when mother comes for dinner tonight."

5. **Denial of Reality:** Polly might handle the threat of Joe and his mother by simply ignoring their presence altogether. She could escape through knitting, joining clubs, or busying herself with unimportant tasks. She simply denies the problem by burying herself in other activities.

Now let's review the five defense mechanisms. In the spaces below, try to identify three examples of how you, your partner, or others have used defense mechanisms in threatening situations.

1. **Emotional Insulation:** Reducing emotional contact with a person because previous experience has caused embarrassment, frustration, or pain. The individual withdraws in order to avoid further hurt or harm. Please give three examples of events that you have either experienced, or seen others experience, that caused emotional insulation:

1. _____

2. _____

3. _____

2. Rationalization: When a person experiences a failure, he attempts to prove that his behavior is "rational" and justifiable, thus worthy of social and self-approval. It is a way in which the ego protects itself by giving an excuse for a failure. This excuse is an attempt to be reasonable. Give three examples in which you have experienced, or witnessed others experience, the need to use rationalization when they had failed and had to give "reasons" for failure:

1. _____

2. _____

3. _____

3. Projection: Projection carries rationalization one step further. It is used when one experiences a failure but then attempts to blame it on another, or when we accuse others of having faults which we ourselves possess but won't admit to. Below give three examples of situations in which you or someone else needed to project away a failure:

1. _____

2._____

3._____

4. Displacement: Displacement occurs when we cannot release pent-up anger with someone, and instead lash out at an innocent party. Usually the lashing-out is directed toward people, animals or objects that are unable to defend themselves. List three examples of displacement that you have observed happening to you or to others:

1._____

2._____

3._____

5. Denial of Reality: Denial of reality occurs when we protect ourselves from something unpleasant by refusing to recognize it or face it for what it is. Another way to deny reality is to show concern for insignificant things, or things unrelated to the real problem. List below three instances in which you or someone else has refused or could not face up to a real trauma or difficulty.

1._____

2._____

3._____

Since defense mechanisms are spontaneous and unconscious we are not immediately aware of them. It is only afterward, when we feel safer, that we look back and recognize the unreal nature of our response. Generally it is helpful to know that if we are real and understanding, we will have less need to be defensive; and that we should try to accept and understand an accusation on face value and from our partner's viewpoint. Refusing to accept or understand a statement only leads to more defensiveness.

Chapter 7

Understanding Others

Being real, open and non-defensive creates the best climate for understanding ourselves and others. This kind of understanding is called empathy and is essential for a good relationship with others.

Basically empathy means that we try to understand what it's like to be that other person. We try to put ourselves in another's shoes. By so doing we acquire a sensitivity and a willingness to accept that person's feelings without judging them.

Empathy is easy to achieve when we agree with what is being said, but hard to achieve when we disagree. However, our goal is always to understand, whether we agree or not. In this way we show the other person that we are open to whatever he or she is saying, that we are really listening. Empathy helps partners come closer together through understanding.

I know that whenever I experience this understanding from someone, I feel closer to that person and can be more spontaneous and warm in the relationship.

Perhaps an example will add to our understanding of empathy in a relationship. The following illustrates how a lack of empathy brought difficulties into the marriage. A meeting with a couple named Bill and Susan went roughly as follows:

Doctor: It's my understanding, Bill and Susan, that you've come to see me because you're having some problems in your marriage. Can you tell me what these problems are as you see them?

Bill: Do you want me to tell you how I see them, or do you
           want Susan to tell you how she sees them? Who's to go
           first?

Doctor: It really doesn't make any difference who goes first. You
           will each get a chance to speak about whatever issues you
           choose, and we'll just simply try to have a three-way
           conversation.

Susan: Well, Bill, I think I'd rather have you talk first.

Bill: O.K. That gives you a chance to shoot me down, but
           we're here to get help so I'll start. Well, Doc, Susan and
           I have been married for five years. We knew each other
           in high school, but we didn't start dating seriously until
           we were both out of college. I recall that I was very
           happy when I met her and learned that she was
           unmarried. She was receptive to our seeing each other
           more often. Susan majored in occupational therapy and
           was working in a nursing home in one of the suburbs. As
           I look back on it now, I get the feeling that in this kind
           of work she was in a position to tell people what to do,
           and it became a habit with her. I didn't realize it at the
           time, but I sure realize it now. I find her to be very
           bossy, crabby, and just plain not much fun to be around.
           What makes me angry is that she has everything that a
           married woman could want. I make good money, and
           she has not had to work since we were married. I might
           add, incidentally, that she quit work at my insistence.
           I've always felt that a woman's place is in the home, and
           the husband's job is to provide a home which is well-
           furnished and in a good neighborhood. From the very
           beginning of our marriage, Susan started making
           demands that I thought unreasonable.

           For example, she said that we ought to have children
           since she was bored to death around the house by herself.
           I remember that we had agreed to wait on having
           children until we got to know each other better and it
           was more convenient for us to have children around. You
           see, I'm in a position with a firm that is looking for
           talented young men to fill in new spots that come up as

the company expands. The competition for these jobs is very keen, and I feel Susan and I have to be available for all social functions and be ready to travel as a couple to various business meetings. If we have children now, we'll be tied down and that could hurt my career. As a matter of fact, I think having children at all will interfere with my career.

I get the distinct feeling that Susan doesn't appreciate me, my work, and everything I do to provide her with a home. Of late nothing pleases her. I guess the last straw was her refusal to go on a recent business trip with me. I got pretty mad and told her that if she couldn't cooperate anymore there was no use in our remaining married. When a wife won't help her husband, then what's the use of having a wife?

Doctor: Well, I guess, Susan, you've heard what Bill has said. I wonder if you would tell us how you see things.

Susan: Well, obviously I think Bill has missed the whole boat on marriage. As a matter of fact, I get the feeling that Bill must have courted some other woman when he talks about our not wanting children in our marriage. That was the only reason I quit my job. I loved what I was doing, felt very needed by the people I was able to help. Quitting that job has left a real void in my life. Before we were married, I told him that I would have to have some outlet for my need to be of help other than his great drive to become president of the company.

I know now that Bill just placated me and really never intended to have children. All he wanted in a wife was a servant, a caretaker, a sex partner, and an image to parade before his colleagues. He certainly does provide us with a great and beautiful home in a nice location. But this is another showpiece for Bill. He really doesn't enjoy the home; he enjoys showing the home. The old image routine again.

It boils down to this. I don't think Bill gives a damn about anybody but himself. So after four years of living in Bill's shadow without having my own identity, or an opportunity to use my talents, I've had it up to here (places a forefinger against the bridge of her nose).

Doctor: Bill, what do you understand Susan to have said?

Bill: What Susan says justifies what I've been saying. She is unappreciative, doesn't give me credit for trying to provide us with a good home, misrepresents my intentions, and, in general, acts like a spoiled brat. What she is saying is, "If I don't get what I want, then I'm going to keep Bill from getting what he wants." A very childish idea at best. I know hundreds of women who would give anything to be in Susan's shoes.

Susan: Huh! There's that ego coming to the fore again. If there were so damn many women wanting to marry you, Bill, why did you chase after me? And as for being a spoiled brat, look who's calling the kettle black. Your mother spoiled you so bad that she devoted all of her life to serving you at the expense of letting your father's needs go to pot. Because I've tried to tell you there are things I need to survive, you call me bossy.

And to say that I am bossy because of my professional background shows how little you know about human warmth and love. I didn't tell people what to do; I worked with people, encouraged them to use whatever talents they had to help them through some sort of crippling illness. Oh, Bill, I just don't feel that you're ever going to be able to let other people live their lives the way they want. The whole world has to center around your needs. I feel the last four years have been so destructive for me that I see no hope for the future. (Susan begins to cry.)

Bill: Now we get the crying routine again. Whenever we try to have a discussion at home and Susan begins to feel sorry for herself, the tears begin to flow. I don't know what she expects to accomplish unless it's that she wants me to give in to her. Well, I don't play by those rules. She can cry, whimper, laugh, or do anything she damn pleases, but that won't sway me from what I know is right.
(Pause)

Susan: Well, Doctor, you have now seen the Bill and Susan show. I thought somehow or other that in talking it out in front of another person, Bill and I would come to understand each other better. But as I heard Bill talk, especially his last statement, I have a sense of relief. His true colors really came out. He is going to have his own way no matter what.

To me, this case is a classic demonstration of misunderstanding and lack of empathy. Neither was open to what the other was saying, and certainly they didn't try to understand what was being said. Instead of a dialogue, we had alternating monologues.

At this point it might be helpful to put empathy into some kind of learning model. This model has four steps.

Step 1. In order to be empathetic we must first be receptive to the data of another. This means that we listen to what is said without judging its value, or being threatened by it. This isn't as easy as it sounds because the data can be contrary to our own values. Not being receptive is indicated by statements like these:

A. "Don't tell me any more, I've heard enough."

B. "I already know what you're going to say, so don't bother."

C. "No matter what you say, you'll never convince me that..."

D. "I don't care what anyone says, I know I'm right."

Step 2. The second step requires that we accept the data from another person and try to understand what it means to him or her. We have to set aside our own values for the moment in order to listen effectively. In other words, we must *listen to understand and not to judge.*

The following statements suggest that we have made judgments instead of having listened to understand:

A. "That makes you sound like a very selfish person."

B. "I don't think you should place so much importance on that issue when we have all these other things to consider."

  C. "Why do you let that person get to you the way you do?"

  D. "I agree with what you're saying, but I don't agree with your interpretation."

All of these are examples of judging the worth of something rather than understanding it. Trying to understand creates within us an attitude which says, "I want to take in everything you are saying, and I want to know what it means to you."

  Step 3. Once we have taken in the information and tried to understand it as the sender intended, we should try to give back, or reflect, this understanding. Reflection means that we repeat our understanding of the message and what it means to the sender. The following statements suggest that we have been open to the message, that we have tried to understand what it means to the sender, and that this is our understanding of it.

  A. "I hear you saying that you feel upset by the way you've been treated."

  B. "I pick up a conflict in what you're saying, and this conflict seems to be giving you some real heartaches."

  C. "I get the feeling that you're caught in the middle between these two friends."

  D. "I'm not quite sure what this means to you. Can you tell me once more what you're going through?"

  Step 4. The fourth step allows us to be open to what follows from our reflection. The sender might respond in one of three ways:

  A. He or she might respond by saying, "I don't feel you understand at all what I'm experiencing."

  B. The sender might say, "Yes, that's how I see this situation, and it's becoming clear to me what I have to do."

  C. Or the sender might say, "I feel you've understood in part what I've said, but you've also missed other important points."

At this point, we return to Step 1. We accept the feedback from the sender as it is given, reflect our understanding of it, and seek further information from him or her.

A second example illustrates how empathy improved a marriage relationship. This excerpt is taken from the final meeting I had with Peter and Alice who had, for all practical purposes, resolved their problems.

Doctor: Let me recap what I understand has taken place in our sessions. I think you have gone from making judgments about each other to trying to understand each other. Peter, remember at the beginning when you said Alice was always second-guessing you? Or her statements were, "Peter, I don't agree with you," or "Peter, I do agree with you," depending on whether the situation was threatening or non-threatening? I think you'll go along with me, Peter, that you thought you knew what Alice was going to say before she even said it. And if both of you will recall, we had some very rough going trying to learn how to listen.

I remember in particular the last session, Peter, when you said: "Alice, I really must have been a pain in the neck to live with. I can see now how I came across as an opinionated so-and-so. I never really appreciated how difficult I was to live with. I'm no angel now, and never will be, but now at least I know how important it is for me to be open to what you're saying and what it means to you.

"And I don't feel threatened anymore when you tell me that I have misunderstood you. God, how that used to bother me! Remember one time, Alice, you told me that you found my mother hard to relate to? I will never forget my response to that. I felt that you were crass, unfeeling, nasty, and certainly unfair to me. It's easier for me to live with that statement now. I can see how some of her habits and attitudes are hard for you to take.

"Anyway, Alice, what I think I have learned so far is that if I create a safe enough climate for you to say what you want, and if I listen effectively and try to really understand what you're saying, then as far as I'm concerned, I'm in touch with where you are."

Remember, Alice, when I asked you how you felt

about Peter's statement, you said, "I feel so close to Peter knowing that I can be myself and not be frightened anymore."

At this meeting I would like for us to talk about maintaining this basic understanding. Alice, let me ask you what you think you can do in the future to foster this understanding.

Alice: Well, I guess I'm going to have to be honest with Peter in sharing with him what I'm experiencing in our relationship. Maybe, Doctor, I can give an example of what I mean here. You know that as a child I was taught never to let a person know what I was thinking or feeling. So I've always been guarded in relating with people. I've also told you, Doctor, that I was taught that if I didn't manipulate people, they would manipulate me. So not only was I guarded, but I tended to manipulate people, including Peter. Therefore, I was always insistent in getting Peter to agree with what I said, and what I said was always something to my advantage. As you know, I've found this very difficult to admit, and even more difficult to change. So in the future I have to be less guarded, less manipulative, and more honest with Peter.

On the positive side, I want to be very open to what Peter is experiencing with me. I want to try to encourage Peter to tell me what he is going through, even if he thinks it will hurt my feelings. That's the only way I'm going to be able to grow and overcome my past habits.

I've discovered another thing. When I can be real with Peter and focus on understanding what is happening to both of us, I get very, very warm feelings about myself and about him. I no longer think he is trying to manipulate me and I do think he is trying to understand me. I really appreciate that effort on his part. It makes me feel good about him. It makes me want to reach out to him and say, "I love you for your selflessness." And when I can show Peter this warmth, this appreciation, it helps me overcome my difficulties in dealing with people.

Doctor: Well, Alice, I hear you saying that you've come upon a formula that has helped you overcome some problems of the past, but more important, it gives you a process for growth and development in the future. I really feel good about what you're saying. What about you, Peter? Tell me about how you feel about the future.

Peter: Well, Doc, I guess I can only repeat what Alice has just said. I don't sense much of a threat in our relationship, and that allows me to be more honest. I think my feelings are less easily hurt, and I don't feel that Alice has to say only positive things to me. In our discussions I have come to realize how my mother spoiled me. That doesn't make me love her less, but it does help me realize I've been egocentric. I also realize that I don't want to spoil our children in the same way. I may do other things that are not useful to our children, but at least I will try to be honest with them and try to understand them and love them without overcontrolling them.

I really want to practice this new understanding in my life with Alice. Does that mean we'll never have any arguments or disagreements or low points or frustrations? No, it just means that when these events occur, if we keep listening to each other, we are going to survive these things and use them as steppingstones for further growth. (Pause)

Doctor: It's at this point that the counselor/client relationship comes to an end. In a sense it's a kind of bittersweet event. Separation in good relationships always brings anxieties. And yet separations under these conditions are very sweet because I think each of us has grown and developed through these encounters. That's the best way to end a counselling relationship.

Now we return to the four steps discussed earlier in this chapter. Let's review them. Empathy requires that we:

1. **Be available to the data of others.**

2. **Try to understand what this data means to the other person.**

3. Reflect this understanding in a non-threatening manner.

4. Be open to whatever response is given to our reflection.

The cycle is repeated until deeper insight and understanding develop between the two people.

In order to help you and your partner better understand the role of empathy in your relationship, we have included a series of statements for you to respond to. Please turn to pages 121-126.

Chapter 8

Being Warm

Another important condition required to help two people relate effectively is *real caring* for each other. Empathy, as we have seen, is a mental function; real caring or *warmth* is a feeling function.

Unconditional acceptance is a technical term which describes this feeling of warmth. When we care about a person, and everything about that person including values that are not the same as our own, we have achieved unconditional acceptance. Without this caring, this warmth, it is difficult to create and maintain a relationship since a lack of warmth tends to keep people apart.

A person I remember who showed this kind of warmth was Mrs. Flowers who was in charge of a neighborhood house where I grew up. She seemed to have a magnet in her body that drew all the kids to her. Her warmth radiated like summer sunlight and we were like little plants turning to a source of warmth and growth. The afternoon milk-and-cookie break was a special time. She would sit in our midst and reach out to us in a kind and loving fashion. She simply made us feel good.

Officer Jennings was another warm person. He was in charge of the school patrol system and periodically visited schools to talk with the patrol boys and share stories with them about his police work. His approach was warm and friendly, and the stories he told were a means for expressing concern for each of his patrol boys. We loved to be close to him.

Warmth does that for us. It draws people closer together in a faster way than almost any other experience. In a way, warmth helps the other two conditions we discussed, being real and empathy, to bring about togetherness between people. If we simply look back over experiences we shared with people who displayed warmth, we easily recognize that warmth was the key ingredient that brought us closer. Without warmth, indifference or rejection is likely to result.

You might ask, "If warmth is so important why doesn't everyone show it?" Like genuineness and understanding, warmth requires conditioning and practice. The expression of warmth can make us vulnerable to rejection, and sometimes that is hard to risk.

Psychologists have studied what happens to children when they are not given warmth during childhood. Without this experience they grow up lacking the background for expressing warmth in adult relationships. This need to feel warmth was considered so important that orphanages often bring in substitute mothers to hold and cuddle infants during feeding time. The comfort found in being held and cuddled is critical for later adult expression of warmth and intimacy.

The need to give and receive warmth is very enjoyable to those who have experienced it. When mutually and freely exchanged, warmth draws people together. But if one attempts to possess the other by warmth, the positive benefits are lost. As a result of possessiveness, an individual is unable to be spontaneous, responsive, and genuine in the relationship. Hence, unconditional warmth is necessary for good relations with others.

A common example of possessiveness is the parents who "kill their children with kindness" in order to keep them under their wings. I remember a college classmate who was engaged to a lovely young lady. She was beautiful in every sense of the word—physically attractive, very kind to others, and helpful to those in need. My friend was very much in love with her and said with loud and clear certainty that he was going to marry her after graduation.

He was, however, only able to attend college through the hard work and sacrifices of his widowed mother, and she envisioned that after graduation he would support her. She often said to my friend, "Now, Bob, I don't want you to feel that you owe me anything for having put you through college. That is what your father would have wanted, and that's what I want; I know college will help you to be a success. But you know, Bob, in order to be successful you have to work hard and not be distracted by anyone. I know Joanne is a fine young lady, and eventually I hope the two of you will marry. But, Bob, don't sacrifice your career for marriage so early in life. Stay with me, save your money, and work hard. Then when you're a success, you can get married."

The clincher for her was the following, "You know, Bob, I'm getting up in years. Let's enjoy each other for the remaining few years of my life." What a dilemma for Bob! He was in love, he wanted to get married, yet he had a mother who had dedicated her life to him and didn't want to share him at this time. She attached a condition to her love and concern. Possessive love of any kind doesn't allow the other person to be.

Another instance of possessiveness which ultimately destroyed an engagement involved a couple named Jack and Helen. Jack approached me at a seminar for engaged couples to discuss a problem—his fiancee's need for freedom. Helen had been asked to work as a trainee for her company, and the training would take her out of town for a few weeks. She was anxious to do the training because it would be a steppingstone to better positions with the company, which could also involve travel and separation. This really bothered Jack. He said he didn't mind if Helen worked, but he wanted her to be home and not travel. It bothered him even if she went out with her girlfriends.

Helen happened by while we were discussing this problem and asked what we were talking about. Jack got flustered and gave an answer like, "Oh, we're talking about the pennant race."

I felt that this was a deception that I had to face, so I asked Jack to tell Helen the truth. She was already aware of what we were talking about and said, "Jack is angry because I'm going out of town for this training, isn't he?" Jack admitted he was and Helen began to say how she felt about this possessiveness.

"He is trying to make a slave out of me. He wants me to be around all the time. He even checks with my mother when I'm out. I love Jack very much and want to marry him, but I don't want to be his slave."

The only reply Jack had was a plaintive, "I don't want to lose her."

I asked permission to discuss the problem with the priest who was planning to perform their wedding. We did and I have since heard that Jack broke off the engagement after Helen insisted on attending the training program. Attaching conditions to his love and warmth for Helen destroyed the relationship.

Possessiveness can be harmful even to married couples who declare undying love for each other. I remember a couple who came to my office on the verge of divorce. After 10 years of marriage and three children, their arguments had reached the stage of wrecking their lives. It all began two years ago at a party where John felt that his wife Mary was too attentive to another man. When they arrived home, Mary insisted that this male friend was an old high school chum who had just returned to the city. They had dated during high school and enjoyed each other's company very much. Then they went away to different colleges in other cities and Mary hadn't seen him since. She was both happy and angry with John's jealousy—happy that he cared enough to be jealous but angry that he didn't trust her in an open social event. Then John began openly taunting her about the good-looking girls at his office. If he worked late he would claim he couldn't get all the dictation out on time. Then with a wink would explain that one of the pretty secretaries would stay to take dictation. Mary then began to be more and more possessive about knowing what John was doing. John, in turn, became irritated when she was away from home in the daytime. She was evasive and unclear about what she was doing. What started out as a cute little game became the serious business of trying to overcontrol each other. Unfortunately, their overcontrol did not save the relationship; it created further argument and disruption. At this point they came to my office suggesting that if they didn't get help, they were going to divorce. Each defined "help" in terms of what the other would have to do. Mary said that John would have to be less attentive to the girls at the office and more responsible in how he spent extra time away from the family. John expected Mary to be less footloose and more of a housewife and mother. Their possessiveness of each other began cropping up even in their relationship with the children. They became more demanding and domineering in their discipline, and their home life became very uncomfortable.

These examples are clear illustrations of attaching conditions to our warmth. Now let's contrast it with warmth that is not possessive, that is a freeing experience. It is given freely, no strings attached, and the one receiving it feels a sense of personal worth and love. What a glorious feeling it is to be loved for just being! Such unconditional love offers the individual the opportunity to accept or reject that love without fear of condemnation, coercion, or complaint. In a spiritual sense, this kind of love approaches the love that Christians believe Christ gave to the world.

In order to help you and your partner better understand the function of warmth in your relationship, we have included a series of statements. The format is similar to those presented earlier. **Please turn to pages 127-132.**

Chapter 9

Sex and Sexuality

Like our drive to satisfy hunger, our sex drive impels us to seek satisfaction. However, it also involves a number of other essential factors not associated with satisfying our other physical drives. Strong social, religious and political considerations, as well as our relations with others, all need to be taken into account in the expression of the sex drive. Because of this complexity, the word "sex" triggers many emotional responses.

For example, in a workshop for married couples I once asked "What is sex?" After some silence and a build-up of tension, one young man answered, "Well, to me sex is something that brings heaven down to earth and raises hell." The group laughed at his definition, but the young man was dead serious. So I asked him to explain further. He said, "Sex to me can combine the best and worst of all three worlds of heaven, earth, and hell. It depends on how you use it. When my wife and I have sex as a mutually enjoyable experience, it's like being in heaven. The feeling is almost indescribable in its pleasure and in the joy of sharing. It's as though you almost leave this world. But there have been other times when sex could be called an almost hellish experience. This was particularly true when there was something wrong in our relations with each other and it carried over as a negative influence into our sexual experience. When there were negative feelings on my part, I knew I was taking advantage of my wife by not really caring about how she felt. My goal was simply to gratify my sex impulse for my own pleasure. Interestingly, at those times I felt guilty, remorseful, and just plain lousy."

This description of sex caused a great deal of tension and nervousness among the other workshop members. Some agreed while others disagreed. The interesting point was that everyone joined in with different opinions, but all were intensely expressed. I said this to the group and noted, "We have talked about many subjects related to interpersonal relationships, but this has been the most fervent. I wonder why?"

Again there was a pause before a lady responded, "I feel that a sexual experience is one which makes each person so vulnerable that even to discuss it raises our emotions. I feel that we become very defensive about making ourselves so vulnerable, and when we do take the risk, we want to make sure that our vulnerability is not taken advantage of. When a sex experience is mutually enjoyable, it can truly be a heavenly experience. Likewise, when the risk we have taken is not successful, we get all kinds of negative feelings and feel hellish. Besides, sex is such a personal experience; it's so emotional that it is almost impossible to talk about sex without strong feelings."

We then discussed how values affect a sexual experience. Again, the discussion was avid and opinionated. The group did agree that values may differ but that a sexual experience was affected by values. For example, one woman stated that she could never even think about sex without love. Another man said that he so prized his wife as a person that their sexual experiences were at the peak of enjoyment when this prizing was felt at the highest level. Almost to a person, they felt that prostitution was a degrading sexual experience. The participants expressed different values, but if these values were not honored, their sexual experiences were affected in a negative way. Almost everyone felt that his or her sexual attitudes were formed early in childhood and that they were later influenced by peer pressure, the church's teachings, and by the advertising media.

The advertising media need special mention because of their enormous influence. One cliche that stands out is "sex sells." Every medium, whether radio, TV, movies, or newspapers, shouts that sex is the beginning and the end of the now generation. We are all familiar with the constant urging to buy a product, to fly now and pay later, or that a beautiful body is a goal in life. The techniques used are usually subtle, but sometimes overt, in order to play on our drive for pleasure. This incessant effort pushes sex without consideration of any value other than pleasure.

Remember in Chapter 2 we defined two personality theories? We called one the physical theory which states that our sole motivation is physical pleasure. The second was the Christian theory, which emphasized the importance of pleasure, but stated that our motivation is directed toward ultimate union with God and took many other human values into consideration.

Regarding sexual relations, the physical theory offers physical pleasure as the motivating force. Sex becomes something to be demanded when pleasure is sought and involves instant gratification without concern for other values.

In marriage, sex on demand or sex strictly for pleasure, does not take into account relations with others, values, social and spiritual concerns. It hinders a couple's growth and development.

Some considerations that support this point of view include:

1. Sex can become jaded through overindulgence and hence require variety which may be sought in more exciting sex partners.

2. In the use of contraceptive devices, one of the partners is required to do something personally without the cooperation of the other partner. This can cause a feeling of being exploited.

3. The always difficult goal of making permanent commitments is further hindered by an emphasis on the physical theory. If pleasure is the motivating force, then what does not give pleasure can be discarded. How this works against permanence can be seen in the following example which occurred during a high school talk I gave to a group of senior girls.

One girl asked, "What happens to a marriage if people fall out of love with each other?" Before attempting to answer her question, I asked the young lady what she meant by "falling out of love." She said, "Let's suppose we don't find our sex life exciting anymore. Do I have to go on having sex with a man who no longer is able to satisfy me? I can't see making a permanent commitment when I'm not sure whether our 'love' is going to last."

Similarly, married couples will often say the same thing as a basis for separation or divorce. They have found another person who is more exciting than their spouse. They have fallen in love again, and they use the word "love" in the same sense as did the senior girl.

4. Sex on demand is a physical response to a drive usually separated from more sensitive expressions of other kinds of warmth. (Emotional reaching out, verbal communication of tenderness, and a special prizing of the total person are usually lacking when the lovemaking is strictly physical or strictly as a release for an impulse.)

These four considerations show that, from a physical standpoint, sex is viewed essentially as a male or female function that gives pleasure. As we now begin applying the Christian theory of personality, we must extend the word "sex" to "sexuality" so that we can include the total person in the expression of sexual feelings and values in the married state. The term "sex" considers only the physical nature of the person; the term "sexuality" considers the total person—body, feelings, and values—in a sexual experience.

We must recognize that in the past popular moral teaching created a negative atmosphere for the expression of sex in marriage. Historically, such teaching tended to ignore the tremendous pleasure of sex, and even regarded sex as almost a necessary evil for the continuation of the human race. At its extreme it implied sex should not be enjoyed at all. In recent years, sex has been placed in its proper context in relationship to other goals in life. It is seen as a powerful force that can be used for the good of the human person in striving for an everlasting goal of truth and good. In this perspective, then, sex must be an integrative factor in our lives. Its expression must have values consistent with our ultimate goal. Let's see how this operates in the married life.

Sex must be natural. By natural, we mean that in its expression, the sex act should include physical pleasure, mutual satisfaction, and spontaneity for the common good of both spouses. This requires a profound sensitivity of the partners to each other in this intimate expression of love. Therefore, such sexual activity calls for careful preparation to provide the circumstances—physical, emotional, and mental—which will allow each to be most comfortable.

Each of these deeply personal experiences should contribute to the partners' coming to know each other better. In the Christian theory, knowing a person is the foundation for true, sensitive love. As this love increases through continuing positive experiences, a married couple's commitment to permanency, fidelity, love, and procreation is helped.

I have come to believe that for the husband to know his wife better, he must be ever-sensitive to her moods, feelings and desires in his lovemaking advances, as he should be in all other aspects of their lives. This attentiveness on his part creates in him a growing feeling of love as he sees his wife respond and develop because of his thoughtfulness.

The wife also must be equally sensitive and considerate of her husband's needs. Her continuing effort to foster increasing closeness through her own sexual advances allows for greater spontaneity and creativity in their lovemaking. This total commitment enhances fidelity between the two and creates the foundation for greater knowledge of each other.

As a result of the Second Vatican Council, Catholic writers on marriage have taken a more balanced view of the purposes of marriage, that is, the development of a mature mutual love and the procreation and education of children. An important moral concern here is the attitude of each partner toward having children. A fuller expression of their mutual love can be had through the bearing and raising of children. But to intend that children are not now, nor ever will be, a possibility in their relationship is to cut off a vital means of expressing good Christian love.

Determining whether or not to have a child at any given point is a practical problem in marriage. A number of effective means of controlling birth are available, among them the use of condoms, intrauterine devices, diaphragms, foams or jellies and surgical sterilization. A real breakthrough in recent times was the discovery of the pill, which has offered great freedom and effectiveness to the user. All these methods are usually called artificial, or mechanical, because they involve some outside interference with normal bodily processes. The official church has rejected all on moral grounds, and lately some people have questioned a number of them on medical grounds.

While the discussion of birth control has placed great emphasis on the question of the morality of different methods, it is important to emphasize that no matter what method is used, if the intent is selfish or exploitive, the method used is then wrong.

In recent years, natural methods have been devised that have proven reliable, and if used correctly, highly successful. Interest in them has been generated not only because of moral considerations, but for reasons of human ecology and good health as well. The most promising of the natural means is the Ovulation or Billings method, which involves pinpointing the woman's time of ovulation by the presence of mucus in the cervix. Abstinence from sexual relations is required during the few days of ovulation.

Periods of abstinence, voluntarily undertaken, can have a rejuvenating effect on the relationship between two people, just as sex on demand can lead to staleness. Furthermore, making a decision together, about any important aspect of your marriage and then working together to stick to the path you've chosen, helps build a strong marriage.

Our study has shown how directly an individual's approach to life can affect a marriage relationship.

We have dealt with two approaches which can be characterized by certain conditions. The physical approach is alluring for several reasons:

1. It emphasizes pleasure as an end in itself, and pleasure has great appeal.

2. It is essentially self-centered and releases us from, or gives us a way out of, permanent commitments to others.

3. It says that the future is of little concern because pleasure is to be achieved now.

The Christian or broadly moral approach emphasizes that:

1. Pleasure is desirable, but other values must be considered as well if we are to avoid selfishness and the exploitation of others.

2. Development of the total person—physically, emotionally and spiritually—is critical.

3. Effective relations with others are a part of this development of the total person.

4. Behavior and goals cannot be separated. Each action should be directly or indirectly expressed as a step toward the final goal of union with God.

A couple faces a dilemma when exposed to the pressure which advocates one approach or the other. The physical world is saying "Get as much pleasure out of life as you can because there isn't much beyond that." The message of Christianity is saying, "Pleasure has a place in our lives but it must be a part of our goal: Union with God." The choice is always ours.

In order to help you and your partner become aware of your attitudes toward sex in marriage, we have included a series of statements for you to respond to. Please turn to pages 133-138.

Chapter 10

Money

A famous comedian once said that money cannot buy happiness, but that it does allow us to suffer in comfort. Among other things, this means that money is a tool to be used to provide for our well-being. And for any couple planning to get married, it is an important tool to understand.

Money has so many hidden meanings in marriage. Frequently spouses are unable to resolve money problems because they do not understand the role money plays in their value systems. Or sometimes spouses will look on money as a separate possession of each, a source of independence. Neither wants to use his or her money for joint ventures. Or perhaps an unconscious motivation contributes to a couple's money problems. Sometimes one or the other might, without realizing it completely, substitute material gifts for unexpressed love. They do so when it seems too risky to face directly the expression of love in a more appropriate way.

Money can also be used as an emotional weapon as, for example, when one spouse uses it to control or retaliate against the other, or when a spouse tends to spend in order to compensate for low self-esteem.

The relationship between money, value, emotion and the well-being of a marriage is not a new problem. We attended a planning meeting for the Christian Family Movement a number of years ago, to decide on an agenda for the coming year. Six couples, in the upper-middle-income brackets, were asked to suggest a theme for development in the following meetings. Most suggested money.

As the discussions went on it became obvious the couples were reflecting different value systems about money which led to many problems in their marriages. Each spouse wanted to manage the income according to his or her own values and held on to these values so rigidly that no compromise could be reached. Their money problems flowed from values that were inconsistent and conflicting. An emotional standoff always followed.

Married couples also often find the management of money a difficult task. The problems are more numerous than most people realize. From the best available information, family counselors estimate that money is the main problem of at least 50 percent of the couples seeking help. Yet only six percent of that group indicates that they do not have adequate incomes or have unusual needs. These facts suggest that the amount of money available is not the major cause of the problem. Mismanagement of the money is.

Mismanagement can be caused by a number of things including immaturity about money and its use, or the lack of understanding of the complexity of budgeting and finance.

Immaturity can be seen in the example of a couple whose material expectations and acquisitions go far beyond their income. They spend lavishly, impulsively or carelessly, running up a long tally of debt.

Such a couple gets very little help from the mass media. Advertising subtly creates wants, urging the consumers to buy and possess things they do not need, cannot afford, but are presented as necessary for a happy, full life. Spending money is made easy through the easy acquisition of credit cards, and buying arrangements that urge "Buy now, pay later," or "No money down, first payment next year."

For those who do overspend, money lenders offer a simple solution in the form of the consolidation loan. "Bring all your little debts to us and we'll consolidate them into one easy payment plan." Immature and unrealistic spenders adopt this mentality as an easy way to have and use money, but show little concern for the financial hazards involved in such choices. However, it is many of these same spenders who eventually come to the counselor's office to learn how to handle their money.

And some couples, though they are not irresponsible or emotional, cannot develop and maintain a budget or deal adequately with their family finances. They may lack the skills to work with figures or to shop effectively for essentials like food and clothing.

While money is a continuing problem in many marriages, other couples experience temporary financial difficulties. They may be perfectly good money managers most of the time, but they may have trouble with situations they never thought they would face—for example, a close relative borrowing a large sum of money and then not paying it back; job layoffs; or extended sickness.

The ability to handle money adequately is only further hampered by the complexities of today's finances. The steady inflation of the past dozen years has eaten away at value and spendable income. To save, invest, or even purchase insurance requires a great deal of financial awareness in order to keep ahead of inflation and taxes, and prepare adequately for the future.

For many people, the credit card is a good means of controlling spending and keeping records. It also provides a convenient way to shop without cash, or to take advantage of good bargains when cash is in short supply. Others, however, do not seem to see the relationship between buying with a card and paying later—usually with an interest charge. The overspending resulting from uncontrolled use of cards is so widespread that support and counseling groups, patterned on Alcoholics Anonymous, have cropped up across the country.

Even the long-cherished dream of owning a home may not be as desirable a goal in an era of inflated prices, climbing interest rates, high taxes and insurance.

The use of money in a marriage requires care and caution. The financial knowledge that a couple has today simply may not be sufficient for tomorrow. It is important to keep learning.

And the opportunities are plentiful. Courses in personal finance are available in adult education programs or through continuing education at local colleges. Financial counseling is available through marriage counseling programs, through investment firms or through social welfare programs. Books and magazines abound, dealing with all aspects of money—from investments to evaluation of products for consumers. Trusted friends, especially those who have successfully dealt with similar situations, may provide a couple with good advice or an opportunity to talk through a problem.

Essential to any financial planning is a budget. Couples planning to get married should work out a preliminary budget, taking into consideration income and such expenses as housing and utilities, food, supplies, transportation, personal spending money, savings and investments, medical protection, contributions and entertainment.

In trying to estimate costs they can seek the help of parents or friends, then discuss the budget with someone knowledgeable about money and finances. The couple may have to try several times before coming up with a workable budget.

As we pointed out earlier, inadequate income or unusual need can also cause money problems.

Mr. and Mrs. Jay are an example of a couple having an unusual need. Their problem was not a lack of money, but how to reconcile spending of it. On one occasion they were at serious odds regarding what to buy their son for Christmas. Mr. Jay wanted to buy the son a Porsche because he felt it would reflect his own status and power as a widely known financier. Mrs. Jay objected because she felt that is was grandstanding and that a less sporty car would be in better taste. His need was to show power; her need was to show good taste.

Six percent of those seeking counseling for money reasons reported they had inadequate incomes. One newly married couple we remember had to budget their money carefully since their combined incomes scarcely covered necessities. After the bills were paid, there was little left. The husband felt that their car would be needing a lot of repairs, so they should consider buying a different if not a new one. But the wife felt that they ought to use public transportation instead and apply the savings toward a down payment on a home. Each became adamant—resulting in a standoff. They would not compromise on their priorities.

This brings us to the two-paycheck family, a relatively new development. Like with the couple above, a second paycheck is often a necessity, not a matter of choice. Since each partner contributes to the family income, each wants a say on how the money is spent. This is understandable, but unless they can agree on what is necessary, there is trouble.

In some other two-paycheck families, the wife may be working through choice. She is not as much interested in the money as in a sense of freedom and self-fulfillment. Still, conflicts can arise on how the extra money is to be spent. Should the husband continue to be the sole support of the family? Should the wife's earnings be spent on luxuries which they could not otherwise afford? The additional money will alter their lifestyle. Realistic management of the income will determine if the effects are positive or negative. In general, if the couple spends emotionally or impulsively, the two paychecks will not solve the money problems. They may even compound them. Otherwise the double income can be used in a realistic and positive fashion to achieve the couple's goals.

Money counsellors offer the following suggestions for handling money:

1. **The responsibility for managing money should go to the spouse whose training and temperament are best suited for it.**

2. **Couples should emphasize "our" money rather than "your" money or "my" money.**

3. **Couples should set up goals which are realistic, achievable and flexible.**

4. **Couples should budget their money only as a guideline to spending. They must recognize that unplanned or unforeseen expenditures require budget changes.**

5. **The habit of saving must be established early so that a couple programs an attitude of thrift into its spending habits. Save a part of every paycheck.**

6. **A couple should seek financial advice on how to invest money. Inflation and/or recession make it difficult for the average person to know what is the best investment plan. As the financial climate changes, competent advisors can offer direction.**

You may find it helpful to explore some statements which contrast the two attitudes about money which we have been discussing. You can compare your own attitudes by the way you react to these statements.

Decide and discuss how you react to the following sentences:

1. I attempt to budget my spending to fit my income.
2. I try to maintain a financial cushion for a "rainy day."
3. I set aside some of my money for recreational purposes.
4. I resist impulse spending when I shop.
5. I try to seek the best bargain for whatever I buy.
6. Before making major expenditures, I try to balance cost against need.
7. I control my money; my money doesn't control me.
8. I can spend money confidently.
9. I feel that I view money in its proper perspective; it is neither too important nor unimportant.
10. I don't feel that I need a great deal of money to be socially accepted.

Now decide and discuss how you react to this set of statements:

1. I can't resist a sale.
2. My money never lasts from payday to payday.
3. I simply can't stay on a budget.
4. New styles are my downfall.
5. My credit card is my very best friend.
6. I've never been able to save money.
7. I can't seem to get enough money for a down payment on anything.
8. I don't think I've ever been out of debt.
9. Whenever I get a raise, I usually spend it as soon as I get it.
10. Money is no good until you spend it.

If you generally agree with the first set of statements, it is fair to assume that you manage your money effectively and realistically. If you generally agree with the second set of statements, then money management is probably difficult for you. Since wise financial planning is important in achieving your goals, seek whatever help you need to develop realistic ways of dealing with your money. Try not to become one of the casualties of impulsive, emotional or careless spending habits.

Chapter 11

In-Laws

In-law jokes seem to have always been a part of the marriage scene. We're all familiar with such comments as "The difference between an outlaw and an in-law is that the outlaw takes all you have and leaves," or "Behind every successful husband is a surprised mother-in-law." They poke fun at a relationship which seems to be all minus and no plus.

We do know that in-laws affect a marriage relationship, so couples about to be married ought to think about their in-laws and how they can be a positive or a negative influence.

Each partner has a relationship with his or her own family that is not completely shared by the spouse. Each must be sensitive to this and at the same time realize their own relationship is more important than any others. Equally important, each partner must understand the kind of relationship the different families expect.

Perhaps examples will best illustrate some of the various types of relationships that can surface when two people marry and bring their respective families into each other's lives.

We remember one couple who was married under "ideal" conditions. Mary was the third child in a very close, loving and understanding family. She had graduated from college and was teaching in a local public elementary school. John, who was teaching in the same school, also came from a close, but larger family.

Mary's family accepted John completely and vice versa. John

and Mary were able to establish a home and to relate well with each of their respective parents. The families always had a good time during the holidays. John often praised Mary's family and said how lucky he was to have such fine in-laws. Mary's sentiments were exactly the same for John's family. When the two had a family of their own, their children experienced warmth, affection and love from both families. Mary and John had built-in baby sitters. They were able to receive help when needed from both families and at all times felt secure in their in-law relationships.

This compatibility stemmed from many factors. First, both sets of parents accepted Mary and John unconditionally. Second, everyone in each of the relationships recognized that Mary and John owed allegiance to each other first. Third, each of the families respected the in-law relationship without feeling threatened or experiencing a loss. Therefore, in-laws can be a great help to a couple if the proper attitudes and proper conditions exist.

Sometimes improper attitudes about in-laws create problems that are hard to overcome. The case of Karen and Scott comes to mind. Karen came from the right side of the tracks in a small town, while Scott came from the wrong side. Karen's family belonged to the country club, attended all the social events of any note and generally was considered one of the first families. Scott, on the other hand, came from a family which was poor, had to struggle hard for the necessities of life, and like most people in their neighborhood had very little social status at all.

Scott and Karen met in high school and developed a very good relationship. Scott was a good student and supported himself through school by working in a local fast-food place. He was determined to make something of himself and was going to have to do it all alone since his family could provide little or no help. For Karen, Scott was a cut above most of the boys she dated. They generally had all the money they wanted, their own cars, and very seldom needed to work or support themselves in any way.

As Karen's admiration for Scott grew into a more profound feeling of love, her family became more and more concerned. Her parents would make statements like: "Yes, Scott is a very fine boy and he is to be admired, but he is not our type. His family isn't on the same social level, and isn't as well educated. We would be very hard-put to accept the family in our social set." This attitude angered Karen to the point where she refused to discuss her relationship to Scott with her family, nor was she willing to give up her relationship with Scott because of her love for him. Scott, of course, was aware of Karen's family's feelings about him. This attitude angered him very much but at the same time he could understand how they might not want to "lose" Karen to him. He actually suggested to Karen that they break up in order for her not to be subjected to the pressure from her family.

In fact, after graduation they both went to college in different cities. Their contact was essentially through the mail, by telephone, rare weekends, and vacation time. Each dated other persons throughout their college years but such events merely reinforced their love for each other. Ultimately, after they both graduated, they decided to marry and settled in their hometown.

By this time Karen's family had accepted the fact that marriage was inevitable but could not accept the fact that Karen was marrying below her social status. Scott had achieved the same education as Karen, but the rest of his family was pretty much where they were ten years ago. Therefore, Karen's family would invite Scott to social events but would not include his parents or other members of his family. This enraged Scott to the point where he then refused to accept any social invitation from Karen's parents. This put Karen in a very severe bind. She, of course, would not go to any event without Scott and this brought anger and hostility from her parents. This dilemma began to have its effect on Karen and, therefore, on Scott as well. She became tense, angry, and generally was unable to please both Scott and her parents. This affected their emotional life, their sexual relations and their relationship with their own children. Scott began to drink too much, and Karen began to turn more and more to her children for affection. The marriage deteriorated because of in-law problems.

Of course, there are other problems that couples must contend with in in-law relationships. A wife married to an only son of a widowed mother can possibly face insurmountable difficulties if the mother and son cannot emancipate themselves from each other. This is not an easy task for either the mother or the son since their relationship is partly strengthened by the absence of the husband and father. We remember a case like this.

Tom never knew his father, having been born after his father's death. With a pension she was able to support Tom without being absent too much because of work. She never remarried, had little or no social life, and began devoting all of her time to raising Tom into a fine young man. She was an exceedingly good mother in every respect. Tom loved her dearly and found her a great source of strength and courage as he grew up. She encouraged Tom to date and let him and his friends use their home for parties and social events. Tom was a good student, went on to college, and became a star athlete as well. He was a handsome young man and proved to be very attractive to the co-eds at his school.

During his senior year Tom met Cynthia and Tom's mother immediately recognized that Tom was in love. For the first time in his life Tom experienced a feeling of coolness from his mother. She wasn't as attentive, caring, devoted or friendly. When Tom faced his mother with this new experience, she denied the source of her feelings. She would say instead that she was getting old, wasn't feeling well and was losing her patience over small things. When they decided to get married, his mother's shock and dismay were quite visible. They both knew that she was going to have a hard time accepting Tom as a married man and Cynthia as his wife. From the day of the announcement to the day Tom and Cynthia came for counseling, Tom's mother did everything to pry this couple apart. Her loneliness was devastating and she demanded that Tom and Cynthia include her in everything they did. When Tom and Cynthia became parents, she was forever critical of the way Cynthia took care of her child. All in all, the pressure began to tell on them. Cynthia felt that Tom gave in to his mother too much at the expense of their relationship.

Tom soon became caught between his wife and his mother and felt totally unable to cope with the two most important women in his life. He had deep love for his wife and tremendous sympathy for his mother. He desperately did not want to hurt either. Thus, the in-law problem began to take hold of the marriage. And as Cynthia felt more and more pressure by Tom's mother, she turned for support to her own parents. The sympathy she got began to bother Tom because he felt that they were interfering just as much as his own mother. This is a classic example of a young couple not establishing the priorities of their relationship immediately. This does not mean that they would have to reject Tom's mother, but that she would have to come to understand and cope with a new relationship in Tom's life which superseded any other.

Such examples show how important it is for the partners, prior to marriage, to openly discuss their feelings and attitudes about their respective in-law families. Nothing should be left unsaid about the in-laws so that each of the partners knows how the other feels and intends to relate to his or her spouse's family. We have found that partners before marriage tend to hide their real feelings about their prospective in-laws. These feelings can be both negative and positive.

For example, one young lady said that she didn't dare tell her partner that she really loved and admired his parents. She couldn't express those feelings because her husband had nothing but feelings of hostility for his parents since he felt that he was always the black sheep of the family. The parents blamed him for everything that happened while encouraging a daughter who could do no wrong.

We also remember a man once stating that he was unable to share his real negative feelings about his prospective father-in-law because his partner refused to allow him to say anything negative about her parents. She then took his silence to mean that he liked her parents where, in fact, he disliked them intensely.

Being forced to hold back any feelings that one has about his or her in-laws is very dangerous to a marriage. Waiting to express these feelings until after marriage is generally too late. Prior to marriage each partner should feel comfortable enough to express his or her real feelings, misunderstandings, and whatever dislikes he or she may experience in relating to the future in-laws. That kind of ventilation encourages openness in an area which sometimes is ignored.

Perhaps at this point it might be well to consider 10 statements regarding attitudes about in-laws, and then discuss your answers. Please turn to pages 139 and 141.

Tear-out Section

Instructions

The following sets of statements are designed to give you some vital information on how you think you act, and how your partner thinks you act. The first set is *Subjective*. Your answers indicate how you believe you act. The second set is *Perceptual*. Your answers indicate how you see your partner's actions. Each partner should respond to both sets of statements before comparing and discussing the responses. Respond to all the statements as quickly as possible and without any help from your partner.

Following the statements is an explanation of responses that are in keeping with the Christian ideal of behavior.

Subjective Statements on Being Real

The following *Subjective* statements deal with a number of ways you express *Being Real* with your partner. Circle YES if you MOSTLY AGREE, NO if you MOSTLY DISAGREE, and the (?) if you are uncertain.

1. I seem to hold back things rather than tell my partner what I really think.   Yes   No   ?

2. I get angry with my partner when he or she gives me honest, open criticism.   Yes   No   ?

3. Sometimes I will argue with my partner just to prove that I am right.   Yes   No   ?

4. Sometimes I deliberately say things to upset my partner.   Yes   No   ?

5. I am usually unable to express what I really think and feel.   Yes   No   ?

6. I usually put up a big front.   Yes   No   ?

7. I tend to be too critical of my partner.   Yes   No   ?

8. I often say things to my partner that I do not mean.   Yes   No   ?

9. I often find myself being insincere with my partner.   Yes   No   ?

10. I often pretend to understand my partner when I really do not.   Yes   No   ?

11. I make my partner feel so safe that he or she can freely express current feelings.   Yes   No   ?

12. I consider myself to be a very real person.   Yes   No   ?

13. I show my partner that I really like him or her.   Yes   No   ?

14. I can express my negative feelings to my partner.   Yes   No   ?

15. I am very obvious in showing my concern for my partner.   Yes   No   ?

Perceptual Statements on Being Real

Your partner would like you to respond to the following statements. Circle YES if your partner acts as indicated by the statement, NO if he or she seldom acts in that manner, and the (?) if he or she sometimes does and sometimes does not act according to the statement.

Remember that your partner wants to know how you see his or her behavior. Do not hesitate to circle a NO or a (?) if it is the more accurate response. Answering the way you think your partner would want is of little benefit.

1.	My partner seems to hold things back rather than to tell me what he or she really thinks.	Yes	No	?
2.	My partner gets angry with me when I give him or her honest, open criticism.	Yes	No	?
3.	My partner will argue with me just to prove that he or she is right.	Yes	No	?
4.	My partner deliberately says things to upset me.	Yes	No	?
5.	My partner usually seems unable to express to me what he or she really thinks and feels.	Yes	No	?
6.	My partner usually puts up a big front.	Yes	No	?
7.	My partner tends to be too critical of me.	Yes	No	?
8.	My partner often say things to me that he or she does not mean.	Yes	No	?
9.	My partner often appears to be insincere with me.	Yes	No	?
10.	My partner often pretends to understand me when he or she really does not.	Yes	No	?
11.	My partner makes me feel so safe that I can freely express my current feelings.	Yes	No	?
12.	My partner considers himself or herself to be a very real person.	Yes	No	?
13.	My partner shows me that he or she really likes me.	Yes	No	?
14.	My partner can express his or her negative feelings to me.	Yes	No	?
15.	My partner is very obvious in showing his or her concern for me.	Yes	No	?

Instructions

The following sets of statements are designed to give you some vital information on how you think you act, and how your partner thinks you act. The first set is *Subjective*. Your answers indicate how you believe you act. The second set is *Perceptual*. Your answers indicate how you see your partner's actions. Each partner should respond to both sets of statements before comparing and discussing the responses. Respond to all the statements as quickly as possible and without any help from your partner.

Following the statements is an explanation of responses that are in keeping with the Christian ideal of behavior.

Subjective Statements on Being Real

The following *Subjective* statements deal with a number of ways you express *Being Real* with your partner. Circle YES if you MOSTLY AGREE, NO if you MOSTLY DISAGREE, and the (?) if you are uncertain.

1.	I seem to hold back things rather than tell my partner what I really think.	Yes	No	?
2.	I get angry with my partner when he or she gives me honest, open criticism.	Yes	No	?
3.	Sometimes I will argue with my partner just to prove that I am right.	Yes	No	?
4.	Sometimes I deliberately say things to upset my partner.	Yes	No	?
5.	I am usually unable to express what I really think and feel.	Yes	No	?
6.	I usually put up a big front.	Yes	No	?
7.	I tend to be too critical of my partner.	Yes	No	?
8.	I often say things to my partner that I do not mean.	Yes	No	?
9.	I often find myself being insincere with my partner.	Yes	No	?
10.	I often pretend to understand my partner when I really do not.	Yes	No	?
11.	I make my partner feel so safe that he or she can freely express current feelings.	Yes	No	?
12.	I consider myself to be a very real person.	Yes	No	?
13.	I show my partner that I really like him or her.	Yes	No	?
14.	I can express my negative feelings to my partner.	Yes	No	?
15.	I am very obvious in showing my concern for my partner.	Yes	No	?

Perceptual Statements on Being Real

Your partner would like you to respond to the following statements. Circle YES if your partner acts as indicated by the statement, NO if he or she seldom acts in that manner, and the (?) if he or she sometimes does and sometimes does not act according to the statement.

Remember that your partner wants to know how you see his or her behavior. Do not hesitate to circle a NO or a (?) if it is the more accurate response. Answering the way you think your partner would want is of little benefit.

1.	My partner seems to hold things back rather than to tell me what he or she really thinks.	Yes	No	?
2.	My partner gets angry with me when I give him or her honest, open criticism.	Yes	No	?
3.	My partner will argue with me just to prove that he or she is right.	Yes	No	?
4.	My partner deliberately says things to upset me.	Yes	No	?
5.	My partner usually seems unable to express to me what he or she really thinks and feels.	Yes	No	?
6.	My partner usually puts up a big front.	Yes	No	?
7.	My partner tends to be too critical of me.	Yes	No	?
8.	My partner often say things to me that he or she does not mean.	Yes	No	?
9.	My partner often appears to be insincere with me.	Yes	No	?
10.	My partner often pretends to understand me when he or she really does not.	Yes	No	?
11.	My partner makes me feel so safe that I can freely express my current feelings.	Yes	No	?
12.	My partner considers himself or herself to be a very real person.	Yes	No	?
13.	My partner shows me that he or she really likes me.	Yes	No	?
14.	My partner can express his or her negative feelings to me.	Yes	No	?
15.	My partner is very obvious in showing his or her concern for me.	Yes	No	?

Explanation for Responses to Statements on Being Real

The first 10 responses are scored NO, and the last five are scored YES. This is true for both the Subjective and Perceptual statements.

When responses are inconsistent, you and your partner must talk about how and why these differences exist. It is important that each of you is open to understanding what the other is saying, so that the inconsistencies can be understood and worked through.

Below is an explanation for each of the 15 statements:

1. I seem to hold things back rather than to tell my partner what I really think.
   EXPLANATION: Holding things back when they should be expressed for each other's good may be caused by a threat that one or the other partner experiences.

2. I get angry with my partner when he or she gives me honest, open criticism.
   EXPLANATION: Being overly sensitive makes a person defensive. Such a person cannot deal with the reality of the relationship.

3. Sometimes I will argue with my partner just to prove that I am right.
   EXPLANATION: If one person needs to be right then it becomes very difficult for either partner to be real with the other. They both have to deal with this need to be correct and not with realness.

4. Sometimes I deliberately say things to upset my partner.
   EXPLANATION: If either partner deliberately sets out to upset the other, defensiveness is created. That partner is creating a threatening situation.

5. I am usually unable to express to my partner what I really think and feel.
   EXPLANATION: If either partner is unable to express how he or she really feels and thinks, genuineness is reduced because they have to hold back rather than be real.

6. I usually put up a big front.
   EXPLANATION: If either partner claims or pretends to be something he or she is not, then genuineness is reduced because the partner is getting signals which do not represent the real person.

7. I tend to be too critical of my partner.
   EXPLANATION: If either partner is too critical, defensiveness results because the other feels threatened by excessive criticism.

8. I often say things to my partner that I do not mean.
   EXPLANATION: If either partner makes statements that he or she doesn't mean, then it is difficult for the other to distinguish between what is meant and not meant.

9. I find myself being insincere with my partner.
   EXPLANATION: Again, insincerity tends to distort what the real person is like, and causes others to be guarded in the relationship.

10. I often pretend to understand my partner when I really do not.
    EXPLANATION: If you say you understand your partner, when in fact you do not, or are indifferent, then you may act in a way that is contrary to what you claimed to have understood. Such behavior leads to confusion and the belief thay you are not being genuine.

119

11. I make my partner feel so safe that he or she can freely express current feelings.
    EXPLANATION: Feelings of security and safety allow partners to be spontaneous.

12. I consider myself to be a very real person.
    EXPLANATION: As a person expresses realness in a relationship, each person experiences openness, which in turn generates more realness. If a person considers himself or herself to be real and behaves accordingly, then the potential for realness for each partner is enhanced.

13. I show my partner that I really like him or her.
    EXPLANATION: If each partner expresses warmth a climate of openness and closeness evolves. This decreases the need for defensiveness and increases the potential for genuineness.

14. I can express my negative feelings to my partner.
    EXPLANATION: Negative feelings create a threat. The freedom to be open to expressing or receiving negative feelings promotes genuineness and reduces defensiveness.

15. I am very obvious in showing my concern for my partner.
    EXPLANATION: Demonstrating concern for a partner shows the partner that he or she can be real without fear of rejection. It reinforces realness.

Instructions

The following sets of statements are designed to give you some vital information on how you think you act, and how your partner thinks you act. The first set is *Subjective*. Your answers indicate how you believe you act. The second set is *Perceptual*. Your answers indicate how you see your partner's actions. Each partner should respond to both sets of statements before comparing and discussing the responses. Respond to all the statements as quickly as possible and without any help from your partner.

Following the statements is an explanation of responses that are in keeping with the Christian ideal of behavior.

Subjective Statements on Empathy

The following *Subjective* statements deal with a number of ways you express *Empathy* with your partner. Circle YES if you MOSTLY AGREE, NO if you MOSTLY DISAGREE, and the (?) if you are uncertain.

1.	I generally understand my partner.	Yes	No	?
2.	I can usually understand how my partner sees things.	Yes	No	?
3.	Even when my partner can't quite say what he or she feels, I generally know what he or she is feeling.	Yes	No	?
4.	I can help my partner know how he or she feels by describing these feelings without making judgments.	Yes	No	?
5.	In holding a conversation with my partner, I am able to follow almost every feeling that he or she expresses.	Yes	No	?
6.	I am generally able to use the right words when I try to show understanding of my partner's feelings.	Yes	No	?
7.	I can usually judge my partner's feelings accurately.	Yes	No	?
8.	I can often lead my partner into talking about some of his or her deepest feelings.	Yes	No	?
9.	I can often help my partner by pointing up feelings that he or she may be unaware of.	Yes	No	?
10.	I usually know how my partner feels by how he or she looks.	Yes	No	?
11.	I know what it feels like to have been hurt emotionally.	Yes	No	?
12.	I never belittle my partner's personal concerns.	Yes	No	?
13.	I find it easy to talk to my partner.	Yes	No	?
14.	I try very hard to pay attention to my partner, and want to get involved with his or her problems.	Yes	No	?
15.	Understanding my partner is very important to me.	Yes	No	?

Perceptual Statements on Empathy

Your partner would like you to respond to the following statements. Circle YES if your partner acts as indicated by the statements, NO if he or she seldom acts in that manner, and the (?) if he or she sometimes does and sometimes does not act according to the statement.

Remember that your partner wants to know how you see his or her behavior. Do not hesitate to circle a NO or a (?) if it is the more accurate response. Answering the way you think your partner would want is of little benefit.

1.	My partner generally understands me.	Yes	No	?
2.	My partner usually understands how I see things.	Yes	No	?
3.	Even when I can't quite say what I feel, my partner generally knows what I am feeling.	Yes	No	?
4.	My partner helps me know how I feel by describing my feelings without making judgments.	Yes	No	?
5.	In holding a conversation with me, my partner is able to follow almost every feeling that I express.	Yes	No	?
6.	My partner is generally able to use the right words when he or she tries to show understanding of my feelings.	Yes	No	?
7.	Whatever my partner says usually fits right in with what I am feeling.	Yes	No	?
8.	My partner can often lead me into talking about some of my deepest feelings.	Yes	No	?
9.	My partner can often help me by pointing up feelings that I may be unaware of.	Yes	No	?
10.	My partner usually knows how I feel by how I look.	Yes	No	?
11.	My partner knows what it feels like to have been hurt emotionally.	Yes	No	?
12.	My partner never belittles my personal concerns.	Yes	No	?
13.	My partner finds it easy to talk to me.	Yes	No	?
14.	My partner tries very hard to pay attention to me, and wants to get involved with my problems.	Yes	No	?
15.	Understanding me is very important to my partner.	Yes	No	?

Instructions

The following sets of statements are designed to give you some vital information on how you think you act, and how your partner thinks you act. The first set is *Subjective*. Your answers indicate how you believe you act. The second set is *Perceptual*. Your answers indicate how you see your partner's actions. Each partner should respond to both sets of statements before comparing and discussing the responses. Respond to all the statements as quickly as possible and without any help from your partner.

Following the statements is an explanation of responses that are in keeping with the Christian ideal of behavior.

Subjective Statements on Empathy

The following *Subjective* statements deal with a number of ways you express *Empathy* with your partner. Circle YES if you MOSTLY AGREE, NO if you MOSTLY DISAGREE, and the (?) if you are uncertain.

1. I generally understand my partner. Yes No ?

2. I can usually understand how my partner sees things. Yes No ?

3. Even when my partner can't quite say what he or she feels, I generally know what he or she is feeling. Yes No ?

4. I can help my partner know how he or she feels by describing these feelings without making judgments. Yes No ?

5. In holding a conversation with my partner, I am able to follow almost every feeling that he or she expresses. Yes No ?

6. I am generally able to use the right words when I try to show understanding of my partner's feelings. Yes No ?

7. I can usually judge my partner's feelings accurately. Yes No ?

8. I can often lead my partner into talking about some of his or her deepest feelings. Yes No ?

9. I can often help my partner by pointing up feelings that he or she may be unaware of. Yes No ?

10. I usually know how my partner feels by how he or she looks. Yes No ?

11. I know what it feels like to have been hurt emotionally. Yes No ?

12. I never belittle my partner's personal concerns. Yes No ?

13. I find it easy to talk to my partner. Yes No ?

14. I try very hard to pay attention to my partner, and want to get involved with his or her problems. Yes No ?

15. Understanding my partner is very important to me. Yes No ?

123

Perceptual Statements on Empathy

Your partner would like you to respond to the following statements. Circle YES if your partner acts as indicated by the statements, NO if he or she seldom acts in that manner, and the (?) if he or she sometimes does and sometimes does not act according to the statement.

Remember that your partner wants to know how you see his or her behavior. Do not hesitate to circle a NO or a (?) if it is the more accurate response. Answering the way you think your partner would want is of little benefit.

1.	My partner generally understands me.	Yes	No	?
2.	My partner usually understands how I see things.	Yes	No	?
3.	Even when I can't quite say what I feel, my partner generally knows what I am feeling.	Yes	No	?
4.	My partner helps me know how I feel by describing my feelings without making judgments.	Yes	No	?
5.	In holding a conversation with me, my partner is able to follow almost every feeling that I express.	Yes	No	?
6.	My partner is generally able to use the right words when he or she tries to show understanding of my feelings.	Yes	No	?
7.	Whatever my partner says usually fits right in with what I am feeling.	Yes	No	?
8.	My partner can often lead me into talking about some of my deepest feelings.	Yes	No	?
9.	My partner can often help me by pointing up feelings that I may be unaware of.	Yes	No	?
10.	My partner usually knows how I feel by how I look.	Yes	No	?
11.	My partner knows what it feels like to have been hurt emotionally.	Yes	No	?
12.	My partner never belittles my personal concerns.	Yes	No	?
13.	My partner finds it easy to talk to me.	Yes	No	?
14.	My partner tries very hard to pay attention to me, and wants to get involved with my problems.	Yes	No	?
15.	Understanding me is very important to my partner.	Yes	No	?

Explanation for Responses to Statements
on Empathy

All 15 responses are scored YES, in both the Subjective and Perceptual columns.

When responses vary, you and your partner must talk out how and why these differences exist. It is important that each of you is open to understanding what the other is saying so that the inconsistencies can be understood and worked through.

Below is an explanation for each of the 15 statements:

1. I generally understand my partner.
   EXPLANATION: Understanding between partners becomes easy if each is genuine and relatively free of defenses. There is an old cliche which says something like, "I say what I mean, and I mean what I say." All of these conditions help partners to better understand each other.

2. I can usually understand how my partner sees things.
   EXPLANATION: When a person is open to the data of others without judging them, it becomes fairly easy to see things as the other sees them. The frame of reference is the other person. But if we make ourselves judge and jury of information, then to understand how the other person sees things becomes difficult, if not impossible.

3. Even when my partner can't quite say what he or she feels, I generally know what he or she is feeling.
   EXPLANATION: Being open to all levels of communication is critical for empathy. When we are open to messages such as body language, voice tone, rapidity of speech, and stuttering, then our empathy recognizes the feelings being expressed, even though the words may be confused.

4. I can help my partner know how he or she feels by describing these feelings without making judgments.
   EXPLANATION: Understanding is made easier by using the right words in describing others' feelings to them. When we use the right words, we help our partner become aware of his or her own feelings and recognize the real meaning of what is being said.

5. In holding a conversation with my partner, I am able to follow almost every feeling that he or she expresses.
   EXPLANATION: Sometimes a partner will indicate different feelings at various times in a conversation. The flow of thought is not always smooth and coherent. However, an empathetic listener is able to follow the partner's shifting feelings and thoughts, and indicate this understanding.

6. I am generally able to use the right words when I try to explain an understanding of my partner's feelings.
   EXPLANATION: It is one thing to be in touch with our partner's feelings and another to restate those feelings in understandable language. We should use words that can be understood and at the same time accurately describe the feelings that our partner is trying to express.

7. I can usually judge my partner's feelings accurately.
   EXPLANATION: The empathetic person attempts to keep on target with what is being experienced. We should be very careful not to sidetrack our partner by exaggeration or suppression. Our restatement ought to fit what is being experienced.

125

8. I can often lead my partner into talking about some of his or her deepest feelings.
EXPLANATION: Sometimes it is difficult for our partner to talk about deep, very personal feelings. With our openness to data, empathetic understanding, and appropriate reflections, we help open the path for our partner to express deeper feelings which might otherwise not surface.

9. I can often help my partner by pointing up feelings that he or she may be unaware of.
EXPLANATION: At times a sender may express confusion about what is being experienced. This confusion is often about feelings that are not understood or are suppressed. Our empathetic listening will help our partner become aware of such feelings.

10. I usually know how my partner feels by how he or she looks.
EXPLANATION: Apart from listening to the words being expressed, we can pick up signals from our partner by noticing how he or she looks. The eyes, the mouth, the hang of the head, and the body stance can give us clues in knowing how our partner feels. The empathetic person tries to match the words with how the partner looks to better understand his or her feelings.

11. I know what it feels like to have been hurt emotionally.
EXPLANATION: To have experienced emotional hurt gives us a certain validity in understanding the hurts of others. We can truly say, "I really know what you are experiencing." Such empathetic understanding gives a sense of relief to the hurting person—they are not alone or unique in the experience.

12. I never belittle my partner's personal concerns.
EXPLANATION: Personal concerns must be understood as such by any listener. To "kid" about, or to belittle, another's personal cares is crass and unfeeling. An empathetic listener shows the sender that his or her concerns are indeed important. Understanding aids in dealing with personal concerns.

13. I find it easy to talk to my partner.
EXPLANATION: In order to be empathetic, a listener must feel comfortable in a relationship. Discomfort creates difficulty in sending as well as receiving messages. Therefore, one necessary condition for empathy is that partners find it easy to talk to each other.

14. I try very hard to pay attention to my partner, and want to get involved with his or her problems.
EXPLANATION: In a close personal relationship, empathy stresses involvement as well as understanding. We show our understanding by becoming involved with our partner's problems and giving help when needed. To withhold such help may make understanding less useful because the partner may be unable to resolve the problem alone.

15. Understanding my partner is very important to me.
EXPLANATION: In a relationship, empathy must be a high priority for each partner, as a means for the relationship to grow and mature.

Instructions

The following sets of statements are designed to give you some vital information on how you think you act, and how your partner thinks you act. The first set is *Subjective*. Your answers indicate how you believe you act. The second set is *Perceptual*. Your answers indicate how you see your partner's actions. Each partner should respond to both sets of statements before comparing and discussing the responses. Respond to all the statements as quickly as possible and without any help from your partner.

Following the statements is an explanation of responses that are in keeping with the Christian ideal of behavior.

Subjective Statements on Warmth

The following *Subjective* statements deal with a number of ways to express *Warmth* with your partner. Circle YES if you MOSTLY AGREE, NO if you MOSTLY DISAGREE, and the (?) if you are uncertain.

1. I am able to show warmth to my partner regardless of what he or she might say to me.   Yes   No   ?

2. I am more concerned about my partner than I am about any other person.   Yes   No   ?

3. Because of my actions, my partner trusts me.   Yes   No   ?

4. I let my partner know that I like being with him or her.   Yes   No   ?

5. I often let my partner know that I appreciate him or her.   Yes   No   ?

6. I make my partner feel that I think he or she is worthwhile.   Yes   No   ?

7. I encourage my partner to share his or her feelings.   Yes   No   ?

8. I make my partner feel secure with me.   Yes   No   ?

9. I foster confidence in my partner by the support I give him or her.   Yes   No   ?

10. I would never knowingly hurt my partner.   Yes   No   ?

11. I really like my partner and show it.   Yes   No   ?

12. I often show that I love my partner by my behavior.   Yes   No   ?

13. I am careful to treat my partner like a very special human being.   Yes   No   ?

14. I respect my partner and show it.   Yes   No   ?

15. I show my partner that I want us to be very close friends.   Yes   No   ?

Perceptual Statements on Warmth

Your partner would like you to respond to the following statements. Circle YES if your partner acts as indicated by the statement, NO if he or she seldom acts in that manner, and the (?) if he or she sometimes does and sometimes does not act according to the statement.

Remember that your partner wants to know how you see his or her behavior. Do not hesitate to circle a NO or a (?) if it is the more accurate response. Answering the way you think your partner would want is of little benefit.

1.	My partner is able to show warmth to me regardless of what I might say to him or her.	Yes	No	?
2.	My partner is more concerned about me than about any other person.	Yes	No	?
3.	Because of his or her actions, I can trust my partner.	Yes	No	?
4.	My partner lets me know that he or she likes being with me.	Yes	No	?
5.	My partner often lets me know that he or she appreciates me.	Yes	No	?
6.	My partner believes that I am worthwhile.	Yes	No	?
7.	My partner encourages me to share my feelings.	Yes	No	?
8.	My partner makes me feel secure with him or her.	Yes	No	?
9.	My partner fosters confidence in me by the support he or she gives me.	Yes	No	?
10.	My partner would never knowingly hurt me.	Yes	No	?
11.	My partner really likes me and shows it.	Yes	No	?
12.	My partner often shows that he or she loves me by his or her behavior.	Yes	No	?
13.	My partner is careful to treat me like a very special human being.	Yes	No	?
14.	My partner respects me and shows it.	Yes	No	?
15.	My partner shows me that he or she wants us to be very close friends.	Yes	No	?

Instructions

The following sets of statements are designed to give you some vital information on how you think you act, and how your partner thinks you act. The first set is *Subjective.* Your answers indicate how you believe you act. The second set is *Perceptual.* Your answers indicate how you see your partner's actions. Each partner should respond to both sets of statements before comparing and discussing the responses. Respond to all the statements as quickly as possible and without any help from your partner.

Following the statements is an explanation of responses that are in keeping with the Christian ideal of behavior.

Subjective Statements on Warmth

The following *Subjective* statements deal with a number of ways to express *Warmth* with your partner. Circle YES if you MOSTLY AGREE, NO if you MOSTLY DISAGREE, and the (?) if you are uncertain.

1.	I am able to show warmth to my partner regardless of what he or she might say to me.	Yes	No	?
2.	I am more concerned about my partner than I am about any other person.	Yes	No	?
3.	Because of my actions, my partner trusts me.	Yes	No	?
4.	I let my partner know that I like being with him or her.	Yes	No	?
5.	I often let my partner know that I appreciate him or her.	Yes	No	?
6.	I make my partner feel that I think he or she is worthwhile.	Yes	No	?
7.	I encourage my partner to share his or her feelings.	Yes	No	?
8.	I make my partner feel secure with me.	Yes	No	?
9.	I foster confidence in my partner by the support I give him or her.	Yes	No	?
10.	I would never knowingly hurt my partner.	Yes	No	?
11.	I really like my partner and show it.	Yes	No	?
12.	I often show that I love my partner by my behavior.	Yes	No	?
13.	I am careful to treat my partner like a very special human being.	Yes	No	?
14.	I respect my partner and show it.	Yes	No	?
15.	I show my partner that I want us to be very close friends.	Yes	No	?

Perceptual Statements on Warmth

Your partner would like you to respond to the following statements. Circle YES if your partner acts as indicated by the statement, NO if he or she seldom acts in that manner, and the (?) if he or she sometimes does and sometimes does not act according to the statement.

Remember that your partner wants to know how you see his or her behavior. Do not hesitate to circle a NO or a (?) if it is the more accurate response. Answering the way you think your partner would want is of little benefit.

1. My partner is able to show warmth to me regardless of what I might say to him or her.   Yes   No   ?

2. My partner is more concerned about me than about any other person.   Yes   No   ?

3. Because of his or her actions, I can trust my partner.   Yes   No   ?

4. My partner lets me know that he or she likes being with me.   Yes   No   ?

5. My partner often lets me know that he or she appreciates me.   Yes   No   ?

6. My partner believes that I am worthwhile.   Yes   No   ?

7. My partner encourages me to share my feelings.   Yes   No   ?

8. My partner makes me feel secure with him or her.   Yes   No   ?

9. My partner fosters confidence in me by the support he or she gives me.   Yes   No   ?

10. My partner would never knowingly hurt me.   Yes   No   ?

11. My partner really likes me and shows it.   Yes   No   ?

12. My partner often shows that he or she loves me by his or her behavior.   Yes   No   ?

13. My partner is careful to treat me like a very special human being.   Yes   No   ?

14. My partner respects me and shows it.   Yes   No   ?

15. My partner shows me that he or she wants us to be very close friends.   Yes   No   ?

Explanation for Responses to Statements on Warmth

All 15 responses are scored YES. This is true for both the Subjective and Perceptual rating columns.

When responses are inconsistent, you and your partner must talk out how and why these differences exist. It is important that each of you is open to understanding what the other is saying so that the inconsistencies can be understood and worked through.

Below is an explanation for each of the 15 statements.

1. I am able to show warmth to my partner regardless of what he or she might say to me.
   EXPLANATION: Showing of warmth under all conditions is the ideal in a close personal relationship. Otherwise, showing warmth under selected conditions can be controlling or possessive. Non-possessiveness means, in part, that we give and show warmth under all conditions, especially difficult ones.

2. I am more concerned about my partner than I am about any other person.
   EXPLANATION: In an engaged or married relationship seeking permanency as one of its goals, the partner is shown the greatest concern. One manifestation of this concern is warmth and caring.

3. Because of my actions my partner trusts me.
   EXPLANATION: Trust is rarely given freely; it must be earned. One way of gaining trust is showing genuine concern, acceptance and warmth. These attributes break down barriers, allowing a person to feel secure and trusting in a relationship.

4. I let my partner know that I like being with him or her.
   EXPLANATION: Seeking one's company is a positive indication of caring. By letting our partner know that his or her company is desired, we tend to reinforce the partner's feelings of self-worth.

5. I often let my partner know that I appreciate him or her.
   EXPLANATION: Showing appreciation for a partner is a sign of warmth which keeps the marriage bond full of life. Conversely, if we don't reinforce our relationship through signs of appreciation, it tends to become stale and uninteresting. A popular banner reads,"Do you love me or do you not? You told me once but I forgot."

6. I make my partner feel I think he or she is worthwhile.
   EXPLANATION: A partner feels worthwhile by being supported in his or her efforts. When we give our partner recognition for these efforts in fulfilling responsibilities, that's how we show our care and solicitude. This is the kind of warmth that enhances our partner's ego.

7. I encourage my partner to share his or her feelings.
   EXPLANATION: Sharing of feelings in an open and accepting manner tends to generate the flow of warmth in a relationship. Feelings give zest and keen enjoyment to our affiliations and should be encouraged as a means to give and receive warmth.

8. I make my partner feel secure with me.
   EXPLANATION: If partners feel secure with each other, they can be themselves. It becomes important that each strives to make the relationship a secure one for the other. Security and warmth depend on each other.

9. I foster confidence in my partner by the support I give.
   EXPLANATION: Confidence allows a person to take risks in coping with life. Developing close, personal, intimate relationships is risk-taking. Therefore, if we foster confidence in our partner, it gives him or her the courage to be open and non-defensive. Warmth is one ingredient to help promote confidence.

10. I would never knowingly hurt my partner.
    EXPLANATION: Caring and concern between partners can never allow one to knowingly hurt the other. By so doing, warmth is extinguished and replaced by negative feelings. Warmth can never be manifested in a knowing, hurtful manner.

11. I really like my partner and show it.
    EXPLANATION: Showing a liking for a person means that one indicates a preference, fondness or kind feelings. In a close personal relationship, partners need to show each other partiality, affection and kindness. These are ways of expressing warmth.

12. I often show, by my behavior, that I love my partner.
    EXPLANATION: The dictionary defines love as a strong or passionate affection for a person of the opposite sex. It then goes on to give examples of instances of such feelings. Thus we must show our love by our behavior.

13. I am careful to treat my partner like a very special human being.
    EXPLANATION: My partner is very special because we experience a unique relationship, one set apart from all others. We do this by being more present to one another, by being more sensitive to each other's needs and by attempting at all times to enhance our relationship more than any other.

14. I respect my partner and show it.
    EXPLANATION: Respect means properly honoring the value of another person. A partner's respect is over and above liking and loving. It is shown through courtesies and recognition, and by acclaiming to others our partner's positive attributes. Respect says, "He or she is a great person to whom I gladly give honor."

15. I show my partner that I want us to be very close friends.
    EXPLANATION: Friendship is defined as a relationship in which two people like, love, honor and respect each other. Close friendships mean that the individuals feel so comfortable that their presence to each other is without strain, stress or fear. It is this element of close friendship that is part of our relationship.

Statements on Attitudes Toward Sex in Marriage

Below are 10 statements that reflect *attitudes toward sex in marriage.*
Consider each statement carefully and decide whether it is YES (or mostly yes),
NO (or mostly no). If you cannot answer YES or NO, circle the question mark.
Please answer as spontaneously as possible, giving the first response that comes
to mind. An explanation follows on page 137.

1. I believe that sex should be enjoyed by both husband and wife.   Yes   No   ?

2. I believe that sexual intercourse for married couples is most appropriate and enhances their relationship whenever both are open to the experience.   Yes   No   ?

3. I believe that sexual intercourse requires sensitive preparation and mutual responsiveness.   Yes   No   ?

4. I believe that a wife should feel free to make sexual advances toward her husband.   Yes   No   ?

5. I believe that sexual intercourse is an extension of other forms of kindness and affection expressed by married couples.   Yes   No   ?

6. I believe it is important that neither spouse ever feels pressured into experiencing sex.   Yes   No   ?

7. I believe that spouses should feel free and be encouraged to communicate what they are experiencing during the sex act.   Yes   No   ?

8. I believe that neither spouse should ever ridicule the other on any aspect of their sexual experiences with each other.   Yes   No   ?

9. I believe that each spouse must be sensitive to the varying sexual needs of his or her partner at any given time.   Yes   No   ?

10. I believe that in family planning, a couple's mutual expression of love includes an openness to procreation.   Yes   No   ?

Statements on Attitudes Toward Sex in Marriage

Below are 10 statements that reflect *attitudes toward sex in marriage.* Consider each statement carefully and decide whether it is YES (or mostly yes), NO (or mostly no). If you cannot answer YES or NO, circle the question mark. Please answer as spontaneously as possible, giving the first response that comes to mind. An explanation follows on page 137.

1. I believe that sex should be enjoyed by both husband and wife.   Yes   No   ?

2. I believe that sexual intercourse for married couples is most appropriate and enhances their relationship whenever both are open to the experience.   Yes   No   ?

3. I believe that sexual intercourse requires sensitive preparation and mutual responsiveness.   Yes   No   ?

4. I believe that a wife should feel free to make sexual advances toward her husband.   Yes   No   ?

5. I believe that sexual intercourse is an extension of other forms of kindness and affection expressed by married couples.   Yes   No   ?

6. I believe it is important that neither spouse ever feels pressured into experiencing sex.   Yes   No   ?

7. I believe that spouses should feel free and be encouraged to communicate what they are experiencing during the sex act.   Yes   No   ?

8. I believe that neither spouse should ever ridicule the other on any aspect of their sexual experiences with each other.   Yes   No   ?

9. I believe that each spouse must be sensitive to the varying sexual needs of his or her partner at any given time.   Yes   No   ?

10. I believe that in family planning, a couple's mutual expression of love includes an openness to procreation.   Yes   No   ?

Explanation for Responses to Attitudes Toward Sex in Marriage

All 10 responses are scored YES. When responses are inconsistent, you and your partner must talk out how and why these differences exist and try to work toward a basic understanding of how the YES responses relate to greater compatibility in the sexual area of marriage. It is important that each of you be open to understanding what the other is saying so that the inconsistencies can be understood and worked through.

Below is an explanation for each of the 10 statements:

1. I believe that sex should be enjoyed by both husband and wife.
   EXPLANATION: Many myths about sex have to do with a woman's role in sexual activity. The myths say that she is not supposed to enjoy sex, that she should be a passive sex partner, and that she should not experience an orgasm. These myths are no longer considered valid. Instead, sex is to be enjoyed by both husband and wife.

2. I believe that sexual intercourse for married couples is most appropriate and enhances the relationship whenever both are open to the experience.
   EXPLANATION: Since both men and women are to enjoy sex, an openness toward experiencing sex is required. Sex on demand by either husband or wife might create pressure, defensiveness or hostility. When it is forced upon either spouse, it becomes an event which tends to create negative feelings not only for the sex act itself but also toward the entire relationship.

3. I believe that sexual intercourse requires sensitive preparation and mutual responsiveness.
   EXPLANATION: The experience of sexual intercourse is much more than just a physical act. Sensitive preparation helps each to develop a positive mental and feeling response to experiencing sex. Furthermore, the physical act of sex is greatly enhanced by such sensitive preparation, and spouses experience greater intimacy at all levels—mental, emotional and physical.

4. I believe that a wife should feel free to make sexual advances toward her husband.
   EXPLANATION: To leave the sexual advances only to her husband deprives a wife of the right and opportunity to inform him of her sexual needs and desires. These advances are helpful to the husband because he no longer has to guess about her feelings. Both then are able to be real, understanding and caring.

5. I believe that sexual intercourse is an extension of other forms of kindness and affection expressed by married couples.
   EXPLANATION: Men and women respond sexually to different stimuli. Men are initially stimulated by visual factors, and women by tactile or touch sensations. Beyond these initial stimuli, kindnesses and signs of affection tend to make each spouse more open to a mutual movement toward sexual intercourse.

6. I believe it is important that neither spouse ever feels pressured into experiencing sex.
   EXPLANATION: Pressure tends to inhibit the mutual enjoyment of sex. Sometimes one spouse or the other encounters pressures from sources outside the relationship. For example, popular magazine articles set up

137

sexual "norms" to be achieved. When one is unable to perform at these levels, the pressure results in a decrease in sexual pleasure. Couples are best served by developing their own norms through being real, understanding and caring of the other.

7. I believe that spouses should feel free and be encouraged to communicate what they are experiencing during the sex act.
EXPLANATION: With recent advances in sex therapy, the function of verbal communication during the sex act is better understood and greatly encouraged. Such verbal communication makes it easier for partners to feel comfortable in their lovemaking ability. This comfortableness allows each to enter into the experience in a more complete fashion, calling upon a total commitment to mutual pleasure and joy.

8. I believe that neither spouse should ever ridicule the other on any aspect of their sexual experiences with each other.
EXPLANATION: Jokes about sex are as ordinary as pizza and TV. A common occurrence is to hoot down a person who doesn't "get" the punch line of a sexual sizzler. Such reactions are counterproductive to any relationship. In a marriage, such put-downs about sex need to be avoided entirely. Otherwise, the ridiculed spouse will find subsequent sexual activity provoking anxiety.

9. I believe that each spouse must be sensitive to the varying sexual needs of his or her partner at any given time.
EXPLANATION: Sexual needs will vary from time to time. At any given time, a spouse may reflect a new and changing sexual need. Therefore, the partner must be sensitive to these ongoing changes and attempt to reach the partner at that point of need. Nothing is more rewarding to a relationship than the effort required to be in touch with the ever-changing and ever-challenging needs of one's partner. We are really saying, "I love you more now than ever before because I am able to remain close to the always-new you."

10. I believe that in family planning a couple's mutual expression of love includes an openness to procreation.
EXPLANATION: If a couple chooses the Christian theory of personality, then all their activity—physical, emotional and mental—is ideally directed toward absolute Truth and Good. Each action, then, is natural as an expression of their God-centered motivation. Specifically, in their sexual activity in marriage, an expression of love which has only pleasure as its goal is outside the Christian model. Therefore, an expression of love through sexual intercourse must not only involve mutual pleasure but also reflect the couple's openness to the procreation which may naturally result. In family planning, therefore, only natural means adequately reflect behavior consistent with our Christian model.

138

Statements About In-Laws

Below are 10 statements that reflect attitudes toward relationship with in-laws. Consider each statement carefully.

1. I believe it is my responsibility to make every effort to get along with my in-laws.   Yes   No   ?

2. I believe it is important that I feel free to tell my partner how I feel about his or her family.   Yes   No   ?

3. I feel that we should have little to do with my partner's family after we are married.   Yes   No   ?

4. I feel that my partner and I ought to have close relationships with each of our families.   Yes   No   ?

5. I believe that I should feel free to tell my partner before or after we are married about difficulties that I might experience with his or her family.   Yes   No   ?

6. I believe that my relationship with my spouse will be more important than any other relationship.   Yes   No   ?

7. I believe that my partner should put our relationship before any other relationship.   Yes   No   ?

8. I believe my partner and I ought to work through any negative feelings that we have about each other's family.   Yes   No   ?

9. I believe that my partner and I should capitalize on the positive relationships that exist between us and our families.   Yes   No   ?

10. I believe that in-laws ought to be a help rather than a hindrance to a marriage relationship.   Yes   No   ?

Statements About In-Laws

Below are 10 statements that reflect attitudes toward relationship with in-laws. Consider each statement carefully.

1. I believe it is my responsibility to make every effort to get along with my in-laws.   Yes   No   ?

2. I believe it is important that I feel free to tell my partner how I feel about his or her family.   Yes   No   ?

3. I feel that we should have little to do with my partner's family after we are married.   Yes   No   ?

4. I feel that my partner and I ought to have close relationships with each of our families.   Yes   No   ?

5. I believe that I should feel free to tell my partner before or after we are married about difficulties that I might experience with his or her family.   Yes   No   ?

6. I believe that my relationship with my spouse will be more important than any other relationship.   Yes   No   ?

7. I believe that my partner should put our relationship before any other relationship.   Yes   No   ?

8. I believe my partner and I ought to work through any negative feelings that we have about each other's family.   Yes   No   ?

9. I believe that my partner and I should capitalize on the positive relationships that exist between us and our families.   Yes   No   ?

10. I believe that in-laws ought to be a help rather than a hindrance to a marriage relationship.   Yes   No   ?